Toward a national policy on
drug and AIDS testing

Toward a National Policy
on Drug and AIDS Testing

Brookings Dialogues on Public Policy

The presentations and discussions at Brookings conferences and seminars often deserve wide circulation as contributions to public understanding of issues of national importance. The Brookings Dialogues on Public Policy series is intended to make such statements and commentary available to a broad and general audience, usually in summary form. The series supplements the Institution's research publications by reflecting the contrasting, often lively, and sometimes conflicting views of elected and appointed government officials, other leaders in public and private life, and scholars. In keeping with their origin and purpose, the Dialogues are not subjected to the formal review procedures established for the Institution's research publications. Brookings publishes them in the belief that they are worthy of public consideration but does not assume responsibility for their accuracy or objectivity. And, as in all Brookings publications, the judgments, conclusions, and recommendations presented in the Dialogues should not be ascribed to the trustees, offficers, or other staff members of the Brookings Institution.

Toward a National Policy on Drug and AIDS Testing

Edited by

MATHEA FALCO AND WARREN I. CIKINS

Report of two conferences on drug and AIDS testing,

Washington, D.C., October 20-21, 1987, and Racine,

Wisconsin, March 8-10, 1988

THE BROOKINGS INSTITUTION / Washington, D.C.

About Brookings

The Brookings Institution is a private nonprofit organization devoted to research, education, and publication in economics, government, foreign policy, and the social sciences generally. Its principal purpose is to bring knowledge to bear on the current and emerging public policy problems facing the American people. In its research, Brookings functions as an independent analyst and critic, committed to publishing its findings for the information of the public. In its conferences and other activities, it serves as a bridge between scholarship and public policy, bringing new knowledge to the attention of decisionmakers and affording scholars a better insight into policy issues. Its activities are carried out through three research programs (Economic Studies, Governmental Studies, Foreign Policy Studies), a Center for Public Policy Education, a Publications Progam, and a Social Science Computation Center.

The Institution was incorporated in 1927 to merge the Institute for Government Research, founded in 1916 as the first private organization devoted to public policy issues at the national level; the Institute of Economics, established in 1922 to study economic problems; and the Robert Brookings Graduate School of Economics and Government, organized in 1924 as a pioneering experiment in training for public service. The consolidated institution was named in honor of Robert Somers Brookings (1850-1932), a St. Louis businessman whose leadership shaped the earlier organizations.

Brookings is financed largely by endowment and by the support of philanthropic foundations, corporations, and private individuals. Its funds are devoted to carrying out its own research and educational activities. It also undertakes some unclassified government contract studies, reserving the right to publish its findings.

A Board of Trustees is reponsible for general supervision of the Institution, approval of fields of investigation, and safeguarding the independence of the Institution's work. The President is the chief administrative officer, responsible for formulating and coordinating policies, recommending projects, approving publications, and selecting staff.

Editors' Preface

Civil liberties, private sector perspectives, and public health and safety issues are critical in any attempt to establish a national policy on mandatory testing for AIDS and drug abuse. This latest volume in the Brookings Dialogues on Public Policy is the product of two Brookings conferences on AIDS and drug testing. The first conference was held in Washington, D.C., October 20–21, 1987, and the second in Racine, Wisconsin, March 8–10, 1988.

Participants attempted to confront the intense political controversy and public fear engendered by the spread of AIDS and the use of illicit drugs in the United States. Though no single policy recommendation emerged from the meetings, the experts reached some points of consensus on possible approaches to testing that would respect the needs, values, and circumstances of affected communities.

We are grateful to those individuals who participated in the planning meetings and studies that preceded the conferences: William Alden, Virginia Baldau, Walter E. Beach, Karst Besteman, Sally Brown, Bill Butynski, Warren I. Cikins, Mark Cuniff, Lee Dogoloff, A. Lee Fritschler, Haydon Gregory, Dick Hayes, John Hoffman, Nolan Jones, Richard Lindblad, Barbara Littell, Laurie Miller, Milton Morris, Pat Nelson, Sandra Panem, Peter Reuter, Robert Schley, Charles Schuster, James R. Sevick, Robert Shriver, Eric Sterling, Florence Sterrett, Elaine Wolfensohn, and John Zeitner.

We are also thankful for the encouragement of Brookings trustee James D. Wolfensohn to examine the policy issues connected with drug abuse in the United States.

Bill Boyd, Dick Kinch, and Susan Poulson Krogh offered valuable assistance in conducting the program at Wingspread, and Donna Dezenhall assisted at both conferences. Theresa B. Walker edited the manuscript.

Brookings gratefully acknowledges the financial support for the Washington conference by the Botwinick-Wolfensohn Foundation and by the Johnson Foundation for the Wisconsin conference.

Mathea Falco
Warren I. Cikins

January 1989
Washington, D.C.

Contents

Introduction

Drug abuse and AIDS (Acquired Immune Deficiency Syndrome) are the two most pressing public health concerns in America today. More than 20 million Americans use illicit drugs regularly; of this group, 10 to 20 percent are believed to be compulsive users dependent on heroin, cocaine, marijuana, and other mind-altering drugs. Since 1985, use of crack, a cheap, highly addictive, smokable form of cocaine, has become epidemic in the nation's inner cities.

AIDS has also reached epidemic proportions in the United States. As of July 1988, 67,141 cases of AIDS nationwide among adults were reported; in addition, there were 1,049 cases of AIDS in children. The U.S. Centers for Disease Control (CDC) estimates that there will be 365,000 cases of AIDS in the United States by the end of 1992 and 450,000 by 1993.

Both drug abuse and AIDS are the focus of intense political controversy and public fear. Recent evidence that the AIDS virus is being spread most rapidly by intravenous drug users has intensified public concern. Unlike AIDS, drug abuse can often be treated successfully and

Mathea Falco, an attorney in New York City, was assistant secretary of state for international narcotics matters, 1979–81. This introduction summarizes the discussions held at two Brookings conferences on drug and AIDS testing. The papers in this volume by June E. Osborn, M.D., Russel Iuculano, and Norman Zinberg, M.D., draw on panel presentations made at the first conference and were the springboard for discussion at the second conference.

At the first meeting panelists Judge Kenneth Starr of the U. S. Court of Appeals for the District of Columbia Circuit Court, Allan Adler, counsel for the American Civil Liberties Union, and James Stewart, director of the National Institute of Justice, discussed the legal and constitutional questions raised by testing. Representative William Dannemeyer, Terry Beirn, consultant to the U. S. Senate Labor and Human Resources Committee, and Mathilde Krim, founding chair of the American Foundation for AIDS Research, also addressed legislative concerns.

is not invariably fatal. However, the apparent intractability of the drug problem, particularly crack abuse, has made drug abuse the number one issue for American voters.

Though AIDS and drug abuse differ in many ways, they are both currently the subject of widespread debate about testing. AIDS tests ascertain the presence of antibodies to the HIV virus (human immunodeficiency virus) in the blood; drug tests generally measure the presence of drug metabolites in the urine. Political support for instituting widespread mandatory testing for both is increasing in response to public concerns that neither has been effectively controlled.

This paper summarizes the discussions held at the two meetings sponsored by the Brookings Institution to examine the critical issues raised by drug and AIDS testing. Participants in these meetings addressed the legal and political concerns, medical and public health concerns, private sector perspectives, and public policy implications of mandatory testing.

LEGAL AND CONGRESSIONAL PERSPECTIVES

Both AIDS and drug testing pose profound legal questions, which the courts have not yet resolved. The central issue raised by mandatory testing is whether it violates the Fourth Amendment, which protects the individual against unreasonable search and seizure—described by one workshop participant as "the majestic statement of a timeless principle of individual liberty against government power."

Some argue that all mandatory testing is unreasonable as a matter of law or policy. Testing removes individual anonymity, subjecting persons to grave discrimination and stigmatization. Drug testing can also incriminate a person for illegal behavior. Testing does not accomplish the goals of reducing drug abuse and AIDS. Moreover, it is never totally accurate or reliable. These arguments are countered by those who believe that testing has an important role in protecting public health and safety, outweighing the potential harm to the rights of the individual tested. They argue that drug testing can both detect and deter drug use, particularly among those who are entrusted with sensitive jobs, such as pilots and railroad conductors. The courts are now considering these issues.

Although courts have generally held that mandatory drug testing is a search and seizure within the meaning of the Fourth Amendment, they have disagreed on whether these tests are unreasonable searches and seizures and therefore unconstitutional. To determine whether testing is reasonable, the courts have looked carefully at the circumstances of the tests—how they were conducted, whether privacy and confidentiality were protected, what use was made of the results.

In a recent case involving mandatory drug testing of railroad employees after an accident, the Ninth Circuit Court of Appeals ruled that the tests violated the Fourth Amendment because they were not based on reasonable suspicion of drug use. The Fifth Circuit Court of Appeals, however, upheld mandatory drug testing of Customs agents involved in drug enforcement work because confidentiality was protected and no referrals were made to criminal agencies.

The Supreme Court has agreed to review mandatory employee drug testing during its current session. Besides the two cases involving federal government drug testing programs, the Court has recently added a private sector case to its review. The issue involves whether the Consolidated Rail Corporation had the legal right to require its employees to undergo periodic drug tests without first having subjected the requirement to collective bargaining.

While the constitutionality of mandatory drug testing both in the public and private sector will probably be clarified within the Court's present term, the issue of AIDS testing has not yet reached the courts. Mandatory AIDS testing raises similar Fourth Amendment questions of unwarranted search and seizure. Because HIV can be transmitted to unknowing victims in ways that illicit drug use cannot, public health arguments may weigh more heavily in support of HIV testing than they do in drug testing. However, the courts may regard persons with AIDS as a special group—a "suspect classification" like race, ethnicity, and poverty—protected by the equal protection clause of the Fourteenth Amendment.

The Criminal Justice System

AIDS and drug testing within the criminal justice system serves a number of different purposes: to monitor drug use by law enforcement officials; to control offender behavior; and to obtain data on the extent of drug use and AIDS among the offender population. Serious questions are raised by testing in this context: whether the correctional system should be required to take steps not required in the larger society; whether there is any legitimate correctional purpose to be served by testing; and finally, what to do with the results of massive screening.

Drug use by law enforcement professionals is a special case. It is not only illegal but breaks an important public trust and corrupts enforcement as well. Moreover, drug use may impair the judgment of police and corrections officers regarding the use of force in the line of duty. A survey by the National Institute of Justice of thirty-three police departments found that more than three-quarters have drug testing programs and screen all applicants for drug use.

Drug testing of criminal offenders is being used in increasing numbers of states as a means of controlling and monitoring behavior. Research studies by the National Institute of Justice indicate that drug users are much more likely to commit crimes, particularly serious offenses, than nonusers.[1] In addition, those who have been arrested and use drugs commit twice as much crime while on pretrial release than arrestees who remain drug free.

Drug testing has become an important tool in many courts in determining which arrestees will be released pending trial. Proponents say that testing provides an objective, reliable standard for assessing risk, and greatly improves the efficiency of the courts. In addition, regular tests can serve to deter drug use among arrestees, since if an arrestee tests positive while on release, he is then incarcerated. Critics note that the urine tests are intrusive and that prisoners are a captive population who cannot by definition give meaningful consent to these tests.

The Federal Bureau of Prisons gives AIDS tests to all inmates coming into the prisons as well as those who are about to be released. Although the Centers for Disease Control estimated that 20 percent of this population would be HIV positive, only about 2.5 percent were. AIDS tests in three states in which AIDS testing of prisoners is mandatory found a similar percentage—between 1 and 2 percent of the population tested positive. More than thirty states are considering legislation to require AIDS testing of all inmates.

The critical issue for the criminal justice system for both AIDS and drug testing is what purposes the tests serve besides generating

1. National Institute of Justice, "Drug Use Forecast Reports" (Washington, D.C., National Institute of Justice, January 1988).

epidemiological data and whether these goals can be achieved in other, more cost-effective ways. Before massive testing programs are undertaken, the costs must be carefully considered, since scarce resources may be diverted from education and prevention programs. It is vitally important to communicate what is known about AIDS and drugs within the inmate population, both to target resources more effectively and to allay fears of infection among correctional and enforcement personnel.

Congressional Perspectives

Some legislators have labeled AIDS the first "politically protected" disease in American history, because seropositivity (testing positive for HIV) is handled differently from other communicable diseases. Although all states require diagnosed AIDS cases to be reported to state and federal health agencies, only a quarter of the states ask doctors to report seropositivity. In addition, knowingly transmitting HIV is a crime in only ten states, although such behavior is criminal for people with venereal disease in almost every state.

In the November elections, California voters rejected a ballot measure proposed by House Representative William Dannemeyer to impose sweeping new requirements for reporting all positive HIV test results and the names of intimate partners by those who test positive. The measure would have permitted use of the AIDS test by insurers and employers as well as allowed doctors to make the test without the patient's written consent. It would have made criminal the knowing transmission of HIV and increased criminal penalties for rape or assault by those who are HIV positive.

This legislative initiative reflects the belief that testing provides important information that must be available to health authorities and that broadly applied restrictive measures are needed to prevent further transmission of HIV. It also reflects a judgment that certain diseases, which may have been contracted as a result of behavior viewed as immoral, can legitimately subject the affected individuals to punitive measures.

Critics point out that such measures both violate basic legal rights and would be counterproductive in the fight against AIDS, by forcing individuals at high risk for testing positive to go underground. Allowing moral judgments to determine policy will not address the problem of

AIDS but only make it more complex. For example, recent measures to prohibit use of government funds for AIDS education of homosexuals will deprive a very high risk group of information that could change behavior.

MEDICAL PERSPECTIVES

From a medical and public health perspective, the goal of both drug and AIDS testing must be carefully examined, particularly since effective treatment has not yet been found for AIDS and is not widely available for drug abuse. For individuals who test positive, the adverse social, economic, emotional, and legal consequences can be immense. This is particularly true for AIDS testing, where positive results can precipitate suicide.

Purpose of Testing

Drug testing and AIDS testing are fundamentally different in that people being tested for AIDS probably do not know whether they are HIV positive, while drug testing does not provide new information to the person tested, only to the testing agency. From a medical point of view, the major purpose of diagnosing both AIDS and drug use is to bring about change in the high risk behavior of the person being tested.

To do this, particularly with individuals at high risk for AIDS, reliable testing must be made readily available at reasonable cost. Furthermore, counseling both before and after the test by trained professionals is critically important in helping the person understand the disease and the need to change high risk behavior. Testing without counseling has no value and may instead be counterproductive. For example, a person who tests negative but who engages in high risk behavior may mistakenly believe that he is invulnerable to AIDS and does not need to change his behavior.

Accuracy of Drug and AIDS Tests

In recent years, highly accurate tests have been developed for the presence of antibodies to the HIV virus in the blood and for metabolites of drugs in the urine. However, despite the reliability of the technology, careless or negligent laboratory work that leads to inaccurate results has been a serious problem. For example, the U.S. Navy had to reverse all positive drug test findings for a certain number of tests, clear the records, and rehire the people it had fired because of sloppy lab work in one of its labs in 1981. New federal guidelines require certification of drug testing labs by the National Institute of Drug Abuse and impose tough quality controls and frequent inspections.

The problem of false positive test results cannot be eliminated by further technological improvements; positive test results first must be repeated to rule out technological error and then must be confirmed by an alternative test method. No matter how good the test is, or how careful the laboratory procedures, the rate of false positives will be higher in low risk populations than among high risk populations. In low risk populations, like blood donors in Peoria, Illinois, 89 out of 100,000 people tested would test positive, although the real prevalence of HIV among this group would probably be only 10.

Both AIDS and drug tests, even when they are accurate, provide only certain limited information about the person tested. Since the period between infection with HIV and the appearance of antibodies ranges from six weeks to fourteen months, the AIDS test will not identify those who are in the early stages of infection. Nor can the test predict when those who are HIV positive will develop AIDS.[2] The AIDS test provides only a snapshot of the person's condition on the day of the test.

Drug tests, however, provide information on drugs used for as long as a week before the test. Marijuana metabolites may be present for seven days, while cocaine and amphetamines are difficult to detect more than forty-eight hours after use. Opiates can be traced two to four days after use. The tests do not reveal, however, whether the person is an occasional user or a chronic abuser, or what degree of impairment was caused by drug use.

A key question raised by both drug and AIDS tests is how often it is necessary to test the same individual to detect high risk behavior. The tests provide information that is valid only at that moment, or in the case of drugs, for as long as a week before. They do not predict the

2. Based on the San Francisco Gay Men's Study begun in 1978, the Centers for Disease Control estimates a rate of 99 percent occurrence of AIDS among HIV-infected persons, with a mean incubation period of 7.8 years. See K. J. Lui, W. W. Darrow, and G. W. Rutherford III, "A Model-Based Estimate of the Mean Incubation Period for AIDS in Homosexual Men," *Science*, vol. 240 (June 1988), p. 1333.

individual's behavior following the test. Unless they are combined with high quality AIDS counseling and drug treatment assistance designed to change future high risk behavior, the tests have very limited public health value.

Risk of Transmission of AIDS

Active dissemination of established facts about the transmission of AIDS would help dispel much of the public fear of the disease and lead to more lucid public debate about policy choices. Using data from extensive, carefully conducted studies, medical experts now agree that AIDS cannot be transmitted by casual contact. The public is not yet aware of how solid this medical consensus is and continues to believe that AIDS can be transmitted in numerous ways, such as by mosquito bites.

Studies looking at the actual risk of transmission have been made of families providing intimate, daily care to family members dying of AIDS, who do not themselves contract the disease. Health workers who care for AIDS patients are also at very low risk of infection, despite publicity to the contrary. Since 1981, only ten to twenty-six health workers worldwide are believed to have become infected as a result of their work. Except for three nurses, all of these cases involved serious penetrating wounds incurred while caring for AIDS patients. By contrast, 450 health workers were killed worldwide in the line of duty last year, 19 of them by electrocution—a likelihood the public would discount compared with the risk of AIDS.

The dominant means of transmitting HIV is sexual intercourse, particularly homosexual anal receptive intercourse, and needle sharing among intravenous drug users. The National Institute of Drug Abuse estimates that there are 1.1 million to 1.3 million people in the United States who use needles to inject heroin, cocaine, and amphetamines. In New York City, 60 percent to 70 percent of the intravenous drug users are HIV positive.

These infected drug users seem to be unusually efficient transmitters of HIV through sexual intercourse, and along with bisexual men, are believed to be the major means of spreading HIV in the U.S. population. More than 80 percent of women and 90 percent of children with AIDS in this country became infected as the result of direct or indirect contact with intravenous drug use.

The widespread sharing of needles within many drug using subcultures poses very high risks not only for heroin addicts but also for those who casually use drugs. Young people in particular, for whom experimenting with drugs is often a rite of passage, must be educated about the extreme danger of using shared needles, even once. Although one experiment with intravenous drug use may not result in continued drug use or drug dependence, it can infect the user with HIV. Both drug prevention and AIDS education programs targeted toward adolescents should underscore this danger.

How Should Testing Be Used?

Testing can be useful in providing epidemiological data on the extent of AIDS and drug abuse nationwide and among certain groups. National surveys of illegal drug use have relied entirely on self-report data, which probably underestimate the actual amount of use. In recent years, however, drug testing of certain groups, such as prisoners, has provided "objective" information based on urine samples. Mandatory HIV testing has also provided data about infection rates among certain groups, like prisoners and U.S. Army personnel. However, efforts by the Centers for Disease Control to develop a more accurate estimate of HIV infection nationwide through random, voluntary testing of 50,000 Americans failed because more than a third of the people surveyed refused to participate.

Which Groups Should Be Tested?

From a public health perspective, the limited value of testing raises questions of its cost-effectiveness, even for high risk groups. Screening the 12 million people who donate blood annually for HIV is very different from using testing as an individual diagnostic tool. The success of "cleansing" the nation's blood supply may have contributed to the political enthusiasm for using testing to "cleanse" society of HIV.

Premarital Testing

One result of this misplaced enthusiasm is the Illinois law requiring that all applicants for a marriage license show proof of an AIDS test. Since January 1988, when the law went into effect, applications for licenses dropped by 25 percent. The Cook County testing facility shut down because it was overwhelmed by the demand for tests, which made testing unavailable to high risk groups. Thus far, only twenty-three HIV-positive applicants have been discovered out of the 150,000 tested, at great cost. As among any low risk population, the rate of false positives has been high, with severe emotional and psychological consequences for the individuals tested.

The Harvard School of Public Health has projected that a mandatory nationwide program of premarital testing would cost $100 million a year. Of the 1.5 million Americans believed to be HIV positive, the researchers estimate that about 1,300 would be identified through premarital testing, a very small yield for the cost.

Pregnant Women, Hospital Workers, and Patients

The critical question raised by proposed mandatory HIV testing of these groups is what is to be done with individual results. Requiring testing of large, low risk groups of people incurs enormous economic and social costs with no clear benefit. For example, if a pregnant woman tests positive, pressure for her to consider an abortion will be strong. However, clinical data indicate that there is at least a 50 percent chance that the child will not be infected. Although mandatory testing can give the individual woman a more informed basis on which to make her decision about abortion, the same result could be achieved by making voluntary testing for members of high risk groups more readily available at lower cost.

So, too, mandatory testing of all hospital workers and patients, a low risk population, raises the question of what use the results might be. Responding to widespread publicity about possible HIV transmission in health care settings, hospitals have adopted the CDC guidelines establishing detailed precautions against infection.

Prisoners, Prostitutes, and Immigrants

Mandatory HIV testing of all federal prisoners, applicants for immigration, and women arrested for prostitution in a number of states has generally revealed much lower rates of HIV infection than expected.

Thirteen states now require HIV testing of all convicted prostitutes; test results were lowest in Nevada counties, where prostitution is legal and regulated, and highest in large cities where most prostitutes tested also reported intravenous drug use. Testing of potential immigrants has thus far found only six HIV-positive people.

Unlike mandatory HIV testing, drug testing has revealed much higher rates of use than expected. Voluntary testing of arrested felons in twelve large cities in 1987 found much more extensive drug use among this group than previously believed: positive tests ranged from 53 percent of the arrestees in Phoenix to 79 percent in New York. Continuing studies confirm that half of all arrestees, and in most cities, three-quarters, are on drugs, predominantly cocaine and heroin.

Options for Intervention

The intense public focus on the tests has distracted attention from what needs to be done to address the problems of AIDS and drug abuse. Debate about testing has replaced careful consideration of how to reduce high risk behavior through education, counseling, and drug treatment.

From a medical perspective, the main value of testing is to maintain a clean blood supply and, to a lesser extent, to obtain epidemiological data. Being able to estimate the size and configuration of the national AIDS and drug problems should contribute to more efficient allocation of resources and better forward planning.

This information should also focus attention on which groups are at highest risk and in greatest need of education and treatment. The drug testing of arrested felons, for example, revealed a rate of drug use far in excess of the general population. However, at present, there are very few drug treatment programs available within the criminal justice system.

Now that AIDS data are available on inmate populations, mandatory AIDS testing may no longer serve any epidemiological purpose. In fact, such testing may subject those who test positive to discrimination and bodily harm. The state of Iowa, recognizing that the costs of prison testing now outweigh the benefits, recently repealed its mandatory HIV testing law.

Concerted efforts should be made to educate the public about the limits of testing as well as the low risk of transmission of HIV through casual contact. The absence of accurate information about AIDS increases public fear and hysteria and stigmatizes those who test positive, as earlier in the century were those who had tuberculosis or syphilis.

From a medical view, the pressing need is to focus public awareness on the high risks of certain behaviors. Voluntary AIDS testing and counseling for individuals who believe they are at risk should be readily available at low cost. In addition, despite present legal and cultural constraints, programs to reduce the risk in these high risk behaviors must also be considered. The distribution of clean needles to drug users, needle cleaning kits, and condoms is a practical adjunct to educational and counseling efforts to contain the spread of HIV.

PRIVATE SECTOR PERSPECTIVES

The private sector generally views both AIDS and drug testing as a means of containing costs—costs related to the treatment of AIDS and drug abuse as well as from lost productivity, absenteeism, illness, and accidents. Testing is viewed as an important tool in risk classification, which allows insurance carriers to assess their potential exposure for future liability. Testing is also seen as a means to reduce risks in the workplace, and increasingly, as a means to deter workers from drug use.

The expanding role of testing both in the government and the private sector raises serious concerns about employee rights and confidentiality. Testing may also be absorbing scarce resources that would more effectively be used for education, counseling, and treatment programs designed to reduce high risk behavior.

Risk Classification

AIDS testing is of particular concern to the insurance industry because of the high economic risk HIV-positive applicants pose for coverage. Insurance companies argue that AIDS should not be given special status when it comes to underwriting insurance coverage. The companies say that AIDS testing must be permitted as are tests for other serious, life threatening diseases.

Of all the tests used to determine the risk classification of a particular individual, none is more predictive of the onset of major disease than the AIDS antibody tests. For example, out of a standard group of 1,000 persons of age 34 who are in good health, about 7 will die from all causes over the next seven years. From a similar group of 34-year-olds who are HIV positive, more than 200 will die within the same period.

The implications of AIDS testing for insurance applicants underline an important distinction between life insurance and health insurance. Life insurance generally benefits the insured's heirs rather than the insured individual, so that if a person with AIDS cannot obtain life insurance, the potential beneficiaries bear the economic burden of the company's testing policy. However, for persons with AIDS, health insurance is critical if they are to have access to quality health care. Rather than raising the cost of the premium, positive HIV tests are often used as a basis for denying coverage entirely, which effectively bars many people from obtaining adequate treatment.

The issue of AIDS testing as a prerequisite for health insurance arises in the context of individual health policy coverage rather than group plans, which provide 90 percent of the health insurance in the United States. Within group plans, AIDS treatment is covered by spreading the risk among a large insurance pool. In small companies, which are not able to participate in large group plans, or for individuals who are not covered by their employers, finding health insurance may be prohibitively expensive or impossible.

The critical question underlying much of the debate over testing of insurance applicants is who will bear the expense of treating AIDS patients—the private or public sector. The cost of treating an AIDS patient from onset of illness to death is estimated at $147,000. The insurance industry argues that the extraordinary expense of AIDS treatment raises fundamental questions of equity: if all insured people are to be treated fairly, how can the industry allow AIDS patients to be subsidized by the healthy?

In response, it is argued that insurance companies enjoy a special role as a social utility, and they therefore have a responsibility to bear part of the cost. One mechanism for spreading the risk is a surcharge on every policy written to provide a risk pool for otherwise uninsurable people. Fifteen states have created such risk pools, funded by assessments levied on insurance companies. The companies are then allowed to write off all or part of the assessment against their state taxes in subsequent years.

Risk classification for drug abuse has not yet raised the kinds of concerns insurance companies have expressed about AIDS, primarily because private companies have generally borne the expense of treatment. Twenty-four states mandate health care benefits for substance abuse problems; employers pay extra premiums to cover the higher costs. However, as substance abuse becomes a greater problem in the work force and costs of treatment escalate, many companies are attempting to limit their exposure for this kind of treatment expense.

Pre-Employment Screening

Increasing numbers of companies require pre-employment drug testing in order to screen out applicants who use drugs. IBM, for example, routinely tests all employment applicants for drugs. Those who test positive are informed immediately and allowed to reapply for employment in six months. A second positive test, however, bars them from further reapplication.

Some companies, in an effort to relieve themselves of the burden of supporting prolonged treatment both of drug abusers and persons with AIDS, have recently established policies that exclude health coverage for diseases brought on by "life style" choices, notably AIDS and drug abuse. However, these policies continue to provide health coverage for AIDS for individuals who can show that they contracted AIDS through blood transfusions or other "involuntary" means.

AIDS testing in the workplace is not yet an issue, since most companies allow workers who have AIDS to continue working as long as they are physically able. State and federal laws also circumscribe employers' right to require HIV tests of employees. The Vocational Rehabilitation Act of 1973, which affects federal agencies and private employers who do business with the federal government, has been interpreted to include HIV-positive persons within the protection accorded handicapped persons against discrimination. Numerous state laws also include persons who are HIV positive within the protections accorded the handicapped.

The military services now require HIV tests for all recruits and personnel on active duty; the State Department tests foreign service officers and their dependents; and the Peace Corps and Job Corps test all their applicants. This testing is justified in part on the grounds that AIDS treatment might not be available in the countries where some of these employees might serve. It also reflects an effort to protect these federal agencies from exposure to additional expense and bureaucratic difficulties of dealing with employees who might eventually contract AIDS.

It is federal government policy, therefore, to screen for HIV among applicants to certain agencies but not others. Moreover, federal policy allows employees with AIDS to continue working as long as they can, makes discrimination illegal, preserves confidentiality, and when necessary, addresses the fear of other employees with counseling and education efforts.

Safety in the Workplace

Substance abuse can impair mental and motor performance, increasing risks of accidents that endanger employees, and in some instances, the public. To identify such problems, some companies have instituted random drug testing of employees. Other companies test only those whose job performance suggests some drug- or alcohol-related impairment. IBM, for example, tests employees only if their performance has deteriorated noticeably and drug use is suspected.

Concerns that random testing can be misused by employers to harass selected employees have led to stricter legal requirements in some states relating to drug testing. Under those laws, private sector employees can be tested only on the basis of a "reasonable suspicion" of drug use. Such suspicion must be based on measurable work impairment.

Union and employee groups share employer concerns about maintaining safety in the workplace. They note that there are many risks in the workplace that have not been addressed. Drug testing that protects the rights of the individual employee and results, where appropriate, in treatment assistance generally has been supported by unions. However, unions urge employers to consider a number of issues before they establish elaborate and expensive testing programs, including the effect of testing on employee morale, what is to be done with test results, and how confidentiality will be maintained.

Drug testing programs must be accompanied by certain safeguards if employee rights are to be adequately protected. First, employees must be fully informed as to the purpose and nature of the test and of their rights, including confidentiality. Second, the decision to test an individual employee must be based on actual, measurable work impairment rather than potential impairment. Third, a proper chain of custody of the test urine samples must be maintained in order to protect against false identifications. Fourth, employees who test positive must be given the right to contest the result and to request confirmatory testing.

Finally, the company must provide counseling and rehabilitation assistance to respond to whatever drug problem is identified through testing.

Protecting the Public Safety

The tension between protecting individual rights and the public welfare is particularly pronounced in relation to jobs that affect the public safety. Because of their greater responsibility to the public, employers of safety-sensitive personnel have greater latitude to test than employers whose employees' work does not affect the public safety.

Determining which jobs potentially endanger public safety is complex: most people would agree that the police officer and the shoe salesman are not in equally safety-sensitive jobs. However, there might be disagreement over whether to classify the airline pilot, the airline mechanic, and the computer programmer who develops the airplane repair instructions as equally important in protecting the public safety. Some public officials serving in fiduciary capacities, like police officers and corrections personnel, are a clearer case in that they are directly charged with protecting the public. However, other public employees, like water quality inspectors, could arguably be as important in protecting the public safety.

The federal government has defined safety-sensitive jobs very broadly. In May 1988, after several years of discussions with Congress, the executive branch released final details of a random drug testing program for employees in sensitive jobs. Under this program, 346,000 federal workers in forty-two agencies are to be tested. The pending cases in the Supreme Court will address the basic issues of whether these tests are constitutional, and if so, on what basis.

IMPLICATIONS FOR PUBLIC POLICY

The fear and hysteria that surround AIDS, and to a lesser extent, drug abuse, have distorted much of the public discussion of these two problems. Since both AIDS and drug abuse are generally linked with heavily stigmatized groups of people—homosexuals and drug addicts—public responses have often reflected moral judgments rather than rational policy. Efforts to criminalize AIDS and strengthen criminal penalties related to drug abuse are increasing: both the AIDS referendum in California and the new antidrug bill adopted by Congress in October demonstrate this trend.

Underlying Philosophical Issues

Much of the public debate about AIDS and drug abuse reveals basic differences in defining the limits of acceptable behavior. One view, which can be characterized as "zero tolerance," condemns any illicit drug use, regardless of circumstances or consequences. This view also condemns any sexual activity outside the bounds of strictly monogamous marriage. Deviant behaviors are seen as closely linked with one another. For example, Carlton Turner, a former White House adviser on drug use, asserted publicly that marijuana use may lead to homosexuality, and by implication, AIDS.

In contrast, the opposing view, which can be described as "differentiated tolerance," distinguishes among behaviors, acting to contain only those that are measurably destructive. This view gives greater importance to individual liberties than the zero-tolerance advocates, who believe generally that even private, consensual behavior can have a destructive impact on society.

This contrast in philosophy is vividly drawn in the current debate about the legitimate limits of AIDS and drug testing. Nancy Reagan, who has taken a leading role in the war on drugs, has frequently stated that drug users should be considered murderers, because they keep drug traffickers in business. The expanding federal government drug testing program conforms to this view—that illicit drug use is as dangerous to society as drug trafficking and must be discovered regardless of cost and intrusiveness.

Because it both detects and deters drug use, therefore, drug testing serves an important function in protecting the public. Illicit drug use poses a direct threat to the public safety when those in safety-sensitive positions, like transportation workers, use drugs. Further, drug use is closely linked with crime, particularly violent crime.

Drug testing can have a serious deterrent effect on illicit drug use, particularly through massive programs of random testing. Many of those who know they will be penalized in some way by positive test results may be discouraged from using drugs because of the possible sanctions.

Besides its deterrent effect, testing reaffirms the society's normative values against illicit drug use. By detecting illegal behavior, testing can also be an adjunct to drug law enforcement. Drug testing can be used to determine whether criminal offenders are released or incarcerated. In response to critics who argue that such use of testing is inappropriate, proponents of the zero-tolerance view note that testing is a legitimate and effective tool for enforcing the drug laws.

Those who believe that drug use must be differentiated from drug abuse see a far more limited role for testing. They note that efforts to deter drug use through testing and other means usually result in changing the behavior of the occasional, controlled user, rather than the chronic abuser. They point out that occasional users, like social drinkers, often play an important role in teaching others how to use drugs responsibly within clearly understood limits. Without the example of controlled users, the only model for those who experiment, as the vast majority of teenagers do, is abuse. They maintain that this philosophical polarity—of total abstinence or total addiction—leaves no middle ground.

This contrast is also seen in relation to proposed measures to contain the spread of AIDS by providing free condoms, clean needles, and needle cleaning kits. Proponents argue that regardless of the morality, and even legality, of certain sexual and drug-taking behaviors, public health concerns demand that everything possible be done to limit the destructiveness of these behaviors in transmitting HIV. Opponents argue that providing free condoms and needles condones immorality and drug abuse and actively encourages others to engage in deviant behavior.

These contrasting views have shaped the public debate about policy responses both to AIDS and drug abuse. Although there is clear agreement that AIDS and drug abuse must be stopped, this consensus does not reach the more difficult question of how to do so effectively while protecting other values, such as individual rights, confidentiality, and privacy.

Medical Coverage for AIDS Patients

The high cost of treating AIDS patients raises several policy questions, some of which have been discussed in connection with risk classification by insurance carriers. The cost of AIDS treatment can be less than some cancer and heart disease cases; however, with AZT therapy, some AIDS patients are living longer, placing additional strain on insurance benefits. This trend may continue as AZT use expands and other therapies are developed that prolong life but do not cure the disease.

State laws providing relief for insurers covering AIDS patients can raise questions of equity. For example, heart transplants are usually more expensive than AIDS treatment, yet many states do not provide special relief for those patients. Extending the availability of catastrophic coverage may help address this situation, where coverage can be obtained for AIDS along with cancer and heart disease. In addition, efforts must be made to find more cost-effective means of treating AIDS patients than residential hospital care, perhaps through expansion of home-based alternatives and hospices.

Importance of Prevention

There is widespread agreement that the route of the future for containing both AIDS and drug abuse is prevention. Education efforts designed to reach the general public are vitally important. So, too, is education aimed at groups at particularly high risk, like adolescents, homosexuals, intravenous drug users, and people who have had blood transfusions. Direct counseling must also be provided, using highly trained professionals as well as peer counselors who can serve as role models.

The media play an important role in shaping attitudes that influence individual behavior. Yet efforts to move the prevention message through skillfully designed advertising have begun only recently and often depend on donated television time and newspaper space to reach the public.

Other underused resources should be explored to expand the reach of prevention efforts. Physicians, for example, are in a crucial position to act as more than narrow medical practitioners and really talk to their patients about AIDS and drug abuse. They are also uniquely able to put their patients in touch with the health care structure to obtain counseling and treatment.

Special attention must be given to training medical students and doctors about AIDS and drug abuse. Many physicians have been resistant to becoming involved in these areas; others who have been working with AIDS and drug patients often burn out from the strain. However, because the physician is often the only point of contact individuals at high risk will have with the health care system, concerted efforts should be directed at strengthening the physician's role in reaching these people.

Maintaining the integrity of the treatment system is especially important in view of the tendency to criminalize both AIDS and drug abuse. Testing in effect becomes punitive rather than diagnostic when it is used to prevent people from obtaining jobs and to keep them from obtaining insurance.

Mandatory reporting of all HIV test results by physicians, as now required in several states, adversely affects the doctor-patient relationship. It also deters many people who do not know whether they are HIV positive from obtaining the test, and in effect, keeps them away from the health care system where they might obtain critical information and counseling.

Efforts to address the problems of AIDS and drug abuse require continuing flexibility not only because the problems are complex but also because their dimensions are constantly changing. No single policy can succeed; instead, a multiplicity of approaches are needed to reflect the wide variations in culture, values, and circumstances among affected communities. Those who are affected are in the best position to know what programs make the most sense for them. Their voices need to be heard by those who make policy and allocate resources.

POINTS OF CONSENSUS

Although developing specific recommendations was not the goal of the Brookings meetings, several themes emerged that reflected the general thinking of the participants:

—The nature and purpose of AIDS and drug testing must be clearly defined. The relationship of different types of testing (that is, mandatory, random, voluntary, routine) to counseling, education, and confidentiality must be carefully examined.

—All testing, except for anonymous testing, should be accompanied by counseling both before and after the test by professionally trained counselors.

—Voluntary HIV testing based on clear, informed consent should be readily available at low cost to identify persons who are at risk and to provide an opportunity to modify high risk behavior.

—Mandatory testing should be used as a last resort, particularly with regard to HIV, where treatment is not yet available (except for limited AZT therapy). Other less intrusive means should be used to achieve society's goals, primarily altering high risk behavior and obtaining epidemiological data.

—Testing, both voluntary and mandatory, severely strains confidentiality. In institutional settings, confidentiality may be impossible to maintain. Recognizing that circumstances vary among institutions, protocols to preserve confidentiality should be established that reflect state laws, regulations, and policies.

—Testing should be undertaken to help, not to punish. Employer drug testing programs should lead to treatment assistance, just as HIV testing should include intensive counseling.

—Insurance carriers should not be required to bear the total financial burden of diseases like AIDS. There is a need for private-public partnership, as in the creation of special risk pools in several states.

—Priority must be given to educating the public, policymakers, the media, health and insurance providers, and high risk groups about AIDS and drug abuse. Education efforts should be specially designed for each group to ensure that decisions are based on the most accurate information available.

—In view of the complexity of the problems, multiple approaches should be developed. No single model works; strategies to reduce AIDS and drug abuse should reflect the many variations in populations, cultures, and values.

—Testing is only one element in a comprehensive effort to change behavior that places people at high risk for AIDS and drug abuse. It should not serve as a substitute for education, counseling, training, and treatment.

POSSIBILITIES FOR POLICY

To narrow the range of views that were expressed in the meeting, I am presenting three possible scenarios. They include the most expansive and the most restrictive interpretation of the acceptable limits of testing, as well as positions in between. The current public debate contains the same wide variation of philosophical perspective and policy analysis.

Expand Mandatory HIV and Drug Testing

This view reflects the belief that protecting the public welfare in the face of the AIDS and drug abuse epidemics greatly outweighs concerns about individual rights. Testing is seen as a primary vehicle for slowing the spread of AIDS, for deterring high risk and illegal behavior involving sex and drugs, and for identifying people in need of treatment. Widespread testing also serves an epidemiological purpose in revealing the size of the problem.

Mandatory reporting of HIV test results to health authorities and mandatory tracking of intimate partners would be integrally involved in this scenario. Proponents of widespread mandatory testing believe that without reporting and tracking, testing would not have full epidemiological, deterrent, and containment value. Individual rights are subordinated to the greater social welfare, particularly since individuals who test positive are often seen as having chosen their high risk behavior and therefore responsible for whatever adverse consequences may follow. Some would propose criminal penalties for knowing transmission of HIV, which they argue is equivalent to murder.

Testing is also seen as a deterrent of unacceptable behavior. Mandatory HIV screening for marriage licenses, employment applications, and military service, for example, usually do not identify significant numbers of HIV-positive individuals. However, proponents justify the high cost of these tests as protecting vital social and economic institutions from contagion. Proponents also believe that testing carries a strong signal that society is determined to identify high risk behavior and penalize those who test positive by excluding them from principal institutions.

Drug testing also serves a deterrent purpose. However, because of the limited information provided by urinalysis, the deterrence can only be of any illicit drug use within a week of the test. Theoretically, only continuous, random drug testing would identify the regular, controlled user who could suspend drug use well before a scheduled test. Despite these limitations, advocates believe that pre-employment and workplace drug testing, regardless of actual work performance, identifies those who might cause workplace problems or endanger the public safety. The potential loss of employment because of illicit drug use, they argue, can be a powerful motive for changing behavior.

The deterrent function of testing is seen most clearly with criminal offenders. Urinalysis is used in increasing numbers of jurisdictions to determine eligibility for pretrial release and parole. Once released, testing positive results in immediate incarceration. Besides its deterrent value, proponents argue, testing improves the efficiency of the criminal justice system in deciding which offenders are most likely to commit serious crimes.

Require Mandatory Testing in Some Circumstances

This view represents the middle ground between those who believe that widespread mandatory testing is beneficial and those who see it as an unacceptable violation of individual rights. In effect, the benefits of mandatory HIV and drug testing are weighed according to the circumstances and compared with the costs incurred in financial resources and in loss of individual freedom and privacy.

There are a number of situations where, by this measure, mandatory testing would prevail. In relation to HIV testing, examples include cases of sexual assault, accidents involving large amounts of spattered blood, or biting of an enforcement officer where the assailant might be HIV positive. Testing of patients undergoing elective surgery, such as dermabrasion, or surgery that poses greater risk for HIV transmission, might be required. Proponents also maintain that insurance carriers have a right to test to protect other insured individuals from carrying the costs of highly expensive AIDS treatment.

In relation to drug testing, concerns for safety in the workplace and in public safety jobs are balanced against the view that urinalysis is intrusive and of limited value. Some would argue that evidence of any drug use, regardless of work impairment, could present a sufficient threat to the public safety to justify testing. Others would argue that measurable impairment of job performance giving rise to a reasonable suspicion of drug use is necessary to trigger mandatory testing. The discussion is most sharply drawn in relation to jobs that immediately affect the physical safety of the public, as for example, train conductors and airplane pilots.

To protect individual rights, however, proponents of limited mandatory testing believe that safeguards of confidentiality and privacy must be maintained. Those tested must be fully informed about the nature of the test and the scope of their rights, including the right to challenge the accuracy of test results and to request confirmatory testing.

Further, testing is viewed as a vehicle for helping those individuals who are identified as positive. In the workplace, employers often support employee assistance plans that provide drug treatment. In prisons, however, there are few treatment options available for offenders. Counseling for those who test HIV positive as well as for those who are at high risk who test negative can help them understand both the disease and ways to change their high risk behavior.

Permit Voluntary HIV Testing and Eliminate Drug Testing

This position reflects the view that mandatory testing is an unacceptable violation of individual rights and that the costs of testing greatly outweigh the benefits. Proponents would redirect both private and public resources used for mandatory testing programs toward education, counseling, and treatment efforts to change high risk behavior. An exception would be made for anonymous HIV testing of donated blood in order to maintain clean blood supplies.

Some advocates of this view would argue that even voluntary HIV testing should not be permitted, since everyone, not only those who know they are HIV positive, should avoid high risk behavior. Furthermore, the inability to maintain full confidentiality of results may subject the individual to discrimination, economic loss, and social isolation. Knowing that one is HIV positive may also precipitate serious depression and suicide.

However, others would argue that voluntary HIV testing, accompanied by intensive counseling and full legal protections, can be helpful for some people, like those who have reason to believe they might be positive and for whom knowing would help inform decisions on marriage and childbearing. Increasingly, with the development of AZT and other experimental therapies, there may also be medical reasons for knowing as early as possible whether one is HIV positive.

This option would permit no drug testing, except in a few extraordinary circumstances. For example, there may be compelling medical reasons to know what drugs an unconscious person has ingested. Generally, however, information about a person's drug use, other than completely voluntary self-reporting as in national surveys, would not be collected. Both in pre-employment screening and workplace safety, other measures of performance capability would be used, such as health history, past performance, and measurable impairment, if any.

Nor would drug tests be used to monitor and control the behavior of criminal offenders. Resources would instead be directed toward providing easily accessible, high quality drug treatment assistance.

Insurance carriers and employers would not be allowed to require HIV or drug tests but instead would look to other measures of insurability and employability. To share the financial burden of AIDS treatment, and in some cases, drug abuse treatment, private-public partnerships would have to be developed to spread the risk.

Medical Considerations

The panel reviewing the medical considerations of AIDS testing and drug testing arrived at several points of strong consensus. It was agreed that deployment of diagnostic or detection tests must be assessed in the context of well-defined goals for a given testing program. Without clarity of purpose, both AIDS and drug testing programs were exorbitantly expensive and could have a negative impact on both public health and individual well-being. Suitable goals would include behavior modification (usually through counseling) for individuals testing positive for the HIV virus or drug abuse; access to treatment for drug abusers; and limited epidemiologic analysis for program planning and public health assessment of the extent of the epidemics in defined populations.

The panel agreed that such goals were elusive if not impossible to fulfill in an atmosphere of public fear. Panel members also agreed that voluntary testing programs for AIDS should be inextricably linked to counseling and that mandatory use of the test would probably be counterproductive as a mechanism to control an AIDS epidemic. Issues of public safety sometimes could justify more coercive testing strategies for drug testing, although members of the panel noted that the range of detectable test substances was arbitrary and usually excluded alcohol, which is perhaps the most important substance of drug abuse that threatens safety.

The convergence of the two epidemics—AIDS and intravenous drug

Medical considerations were reviewed by panelists June E. Osborn, M.D., dean, School of Public Health, University of Michigan; Marcus Conant, M.D., clinical professor of dermatology, University of California Medical Center, San Francisco, chairman, California State Department of Health Services Task Force on AIDS; John Henning, M.D., Office of Science and Technology, American Medical Assocation; and Steven Shultz, M.D., deputy commissioner of Epidemiology and Preventative Services, New York City Department of Health.

abuse—was noted with special concern, in view of the absolute lack of curative or vaccine options for AIDS and the lack of treatment resources for intravenous drug abusers. The tendency to approach both populations—HIV-infected individuals and intravenous drug abusers —as "cast-off" or undesirable components of society was viewed as an important circumstance that interferes with public attitudes and therefore with public policy formulation.

The use of HIV testing to ascertain the range and magnitude of the AIDS epidemic in the future is clearly important, but the profound public fear and distrust that currently prevail may blunt the efficacy of such efforts. For instance, initial efforts by the Centers for Disease Control to do a well-constructed, anonymous household survey were aborted when it was found that fully one-third of persons asked were unwilling to participate. That response underlines the ongoing need for general public education to allay unreasoning fear and the equally great need to curtail discriminatory behavior against AIDS patients and HIV-infected persons.

Routine or even involuntary HIV testing might be justified in certain conditions, for example, prison settings where local conditions permit the occurrence of homosexual rape or drug abuse, and certain instances of elective surgery. Even then it is crucial that testing be done within a carefully observed ethical framework and that quality of life and care not be jeopardized by the enactment of the testing policy.

Finally, the panel agreed that the consensus positions might change greatly if new options opened in the realm of HIV vaccine or therapy or access to treatment for intravenous drug abusers.

AIDS TESTING

When screening tests become available for detection of specific markers of disease, pressure often arises to put them to use. Such pressure may develop independently of particular rationales or strategies for utilizing the test results, and in the past some screening programs have excited controversy and criticism because they resulted in unanticipated harm without achieving a counterbalancing benefit.[1] Such dissociation be-

1. S. Elias and G. J. Annas, "Routine Prenatal Genetic Screening," *New England Journal of Medicine*, vol. 317 (November 1987), pp. 1407–09.

tween screening activities and outcome is exorbitantly costly in human as well as fiscal resources.

Both HIV testing and drug testing have been advocated as key weapons in the concurrent epidemics of AIDS and of drug abuse; but as in other screening initiatives, it is crucial to assess the benefits of test results obtained against the background of personal and even public health risks that may accrue as an unwanted by-product of the testing programs.

This paper focuses on screening for AIDS—or more accurately, screening for HIV. Issues of substance abuse, illicit drug use, and screening tests to detect abused substances will be dealt with only cursorily, usually when they provide either emphasis or contrast to issues arising from AIDS testing. Although the comparison between AIDS testing and drug testing is a fruitful exercise since it highlights certain issues or concerns, the actual parallels and similarities between the two types of testing are more superficial than substantive. Indeed, while substance abuse can be a crippling and chronic health problem for a given individual, testing detects only a transient situation—whether the results are positive or negative. By contrast, once HIV infection is acquired, it persists for the lifetime of the individual, and while its likelihood of progression to devastating, ultimately lethal disease is not yet precisely known, the odds of serious consequences are sufficiently high that a single determination of HIV seropositivity carries a profound impact for the lifetime of the individual tested.

Because of the recency and novelty of AIDS, a brief review of the known data on HIV infection and disease may be helpful. Aggressive public health screening strategies are commonly justified on the grounds that "there's a lot we don't know about AIDS." Though that statement is clearly correct in the absolute sense, it is seriously misleading. The first cases of AIDS were diagnosed in 1981, and yet less than seven years later as much or more is known about the causative virus and its basic biochemical and biological properties than about any other viral pathogen of man. (See table 1 for chronology of epidemic.) In particular, abundant information exists on which to base sound public health policies.[2]

2. National Academy of Sciences, Committee on a National Strategy on AIDS, *Confronting AIDS: Directions for Public Health Care and Research* (Washington, D.C.: National Academy Press, 1986).

TABLE 1. *History of HIV in the United States*

Year	Event
1960	(1959) First antibody evidence of human infection (Zaire)
	Late 1960s: Probable introduction into United States
1970	Late 1970s: Appearance of AIDS (diagnosed retrospectively)
	Many cases of AIDS-related complex
	(lymphadenopathy)
1980	
1981	AIDS recognized and described in gay men in New York, Los Angeles
1982	AIDS named; recognized in intravenous drug users and their sexual partners
	recognized in hemophiliacs
	recognized in Haitians (male:female ratio 3:1)
1983	AIDS occurs in transfusion recipients
	High risk individuals asked not to donate blood and plasma
1984	Virus isolated at Institut Pasteur (Luc Montagnier)
	Virus isolated at National Institutes of Health (Robert Gallo)
	Virus isolated in San Francisco (Jay Levy)
1985	Diagnostic test licensed: testing feasible
	blood supply screened
	Military screening begun
	Rock Hudson dies
1986	Coolfont conference
	National Academy of Science/Institute of Medicine study (report October 1986: *Confronting AIDS*)
	AZT trials
	Robert Wood Johnson project started
1987	32,000 cases
	AZT licensed $7,000–$10,000 a year
	(AIDS Awareness and Prevention Month)
	All vaccine candidates fail to protect chimpanzees
1988	50,000 cases
	Informational brochure mailed to American households by U.S. Public Health Service
1989	
1990	
1991	270,000 cases cumulative projected (171,000+ cumulative deaths)

The virus of AIDS, now called human immunodeficiency virus or HIV, is a member of the lentivirus subgroup of a major family of animal viruses called retroviruses. That fact has been conceptually useful: knowledge of the biologic properties of other viruses within the group (much of it acquired through basic research prior to the recognized advent of AIDS) has facilitated predictions and hypotheses about HIV and thus accelerated the progress of research.[3]

Among the properties shared by HIV with other lentiviruses are its permanence of infection, the extreme difficulty and limited routes of transmission, and an indeterminate immunologic relationship with the infected host in which *protective* immune responses seem to occur weakly if at all. Antibodies do appear relatively promptly after infection, and they are useful for diagnosis of the presence of infection. However, they seem unable to terminate or contain viral multiplication, and no other facets of the immune response have been recognized to exert protective effect.[4]

Another property shared by HIV with other lentiviruses is a change-ability of the proteins that comprise the outer covering (or envelope) of the virus; this property is usually called antigenic variation, since those envelope proteins are the antigens most likely to provoke a host immune response. This variability of envelope antigens adds to the difficulty of vaccine development, since even if a successful effort were mounted to create a vaccine against a specific isolate of HIV, the virus might change its surface proteins enough to evade the vaccine-induced immune response.[5]

3. Recognition of the close relatedness of HIV to lentiviruses of other species also lays to rest concerns that the novelty of HIV in humans might signify an extraplanetary origin: that is virtually untenable in that HIV is so closely related to its viral cousins that it shares significant portions of its nucleic acid sequences with them and conforms in various ways to terrestrial biologic rules.

4. This critical fact underlies the grim prognostication that vaccines against HIV will take many years to develop if indeed they are ever developed.

5. This ability to change antigens has caused persons unfamiliar with virology to fear that a change in biologic properties such as route of transmission might be equally likely. However, whereas antigenic variation is a manifestation of minor molecular changes, it would take a massive multifaceted change in the genetic make-up of the virus to accomplish the profound biologic alterations needed for new, broader patterns of spread to occur. Thus the concern that HIV might yet become readily transmissible by casual contact has no biologic basis or precedent.

TABLE 2. *Fact Sheet about HIV*

Route of Infection
  Known to transmit
    Sexual intercourse, both homosexual and heterosexual (efficiency varies:
      anal receptive homosexual intercourse >> male-to-female >>
      female-to-male
    Blood transfusion; transfer of substantial volumes of blood (12 dc)
    Transplanted organs, tissues, cells
    Mother-to-child before or at birth (antibody transferred virtually 100%,
      virus infection in infant established in 30–50% of cases)
    Breast milk—frequency unknown
  May transmit rarely
    Accidental needle puncture (health care workers) estimated at 3 per
      1,000
    Laboratory exposure to high concentration of virus in research setting
      estimated at 3 per 1,000
  Known not to transmit
    Intimate nonsexual contact
    Casual contact
    Mosquitoes and biting insects
Interval to appearance of antibodies: 4–12 weeks
Interval to appearance of AIDS: Mean is approximately 7 years (1 case
estimated at 15 years)
Likelihood of developing disease: ≥50%

The central properties of HIV important to this discussion are modes of transmission, the sequence of events that follows infection of a susceptible individual, and the indicators available to recognize that infection. These are summarized in table 2.

Transmission is the key issue for public health programs, and consequently much of public policy relates to testing to detect infected persons. Several strong assertions can be made about transmissibility of the virus, based on extensive data from real-life situations. First, the dominant mode of spread in nature for HIV is sexual intercourse, and the virus can be spread by both homosexual and heterosexual intercourse. While the efficiency of transmission varies (with homosexual anal receptive intercourse being by far the most efficient), the possibility of spread exists in virtually all pairings. Certain "cofactors," especially genital ulcer disease (syphilis, genital herpes, or chancroid) and probably other sexually transmitted diseases seem to enhance the likelihood of transmission from one sexual partner to another.

Transmission by blood transfusion is the single most efficient route, but even then only 90 percent of recipients of HIV-infected blood become infected. Transmission between drug addicts who share needles is presumed to reflect blood transfer, but the situation is less than straightforward as rates of infection vary widely in different intravenous drug user populations. This variability probably reflects different cultural and social factors, including extent of "blood-brother" sharing; access to "shooting galleries" in which injection apparatus is rented and reused extensively without intervening sterilization; and the likelihood that cross-group sharing of drugs may occur.[6]

For whatever reasons, the frequency of HIV infection among intravenous drug users ranges from a high of over 60 percent in New York City and parts of New Jersey to a rather stable 2 percent in Los Angeles and New Orleans. Some European countries show the same pattern as New York, while in other U.S. cities the rates of infection are in between, with gradually increasing prevalence of infection: Chicago and Detroit, for instance, have shown steadily increasing percentages with approximately 10 percent to 20 percent of intravenous drug users infected in the most recent surveys. For reasons that are not clear, intravenous drug users who become infected seem to be unusually efficient spreaders of HIV via sexual intercourse, and (along with bisexual men) they represent the major vehicle whereby the AIDS epidemic is expected to broaden in the U.S. population. Over 80 percent of women and over 90 percent of children with AIDS in the United States became infected with HIV as the direct or indirect result of intravenous drug use.

Transmission of HIV by donated organs, tissues, and cells as well as by blood has been shown to occur. A policy of mandatory screening of blood donors for antibody to HIV has been in place since May 1985 (and of other donors subsequently as the risks of organ and cell donations have become evident). Since testing was instituted, of more

---

6. For instance, it is said that injection equipment is shared only among close friends in Los Angeles, whereas no such boundaries apply along the East Coast.

than 30 million donations, only 8 instances have occurred in which HIV was transmitted via blood.[7]

An infant born to an HIV-infected mother may well be infected, but the likelihood is by no means 100 percent. Transmission of HIV from mother to child occurs in utero or at the time of birth at a frequency of between 30 percent and 50 percent. If one tests blood from infants newly born to infected mothers for antibodies to HIV, virtually 100 percent will test positive because of passive transfer of maternal HIV antibodies across the placenta. It is not possible to predict in the first few months of life which antibody-positive infants are actually infected; that can be ascertained only after several months, either by development of disease or disappearance of antibody.

At least as important from the vantage point of screening policies are the data on failure of transmission. The inability of HIV to spread by any but sexual or bloodborne routes has been resoundingly established in various careful epidemiologic studies.[8] Hundreds of family members who sustained intimate (nonsexual) contact with dying AIDS patients for whom they cared (at home) over many weeks or months were subsequently tested repeatedly for HIV antibody. Not a single person became infected despite sharing of toilets, cups, utensils, razors, or kisses.

Given the number of asymptomatically infected individuals having intermittent contact with the health care system, it is almost equally dramatic to note that no health care worker has become infected in the course of ordinary duty (unless he or she had a personal risk behavior). Transmission has been linked with needle-stick or unusual exposure

7. Two of these donors went to blood banks specifically to ascertain their antibody status, since alternative testing was not readily available. They thought they could rely on the testing program to prevent their blood being used should they prove to be infected. However, their infection was too recent for them to have developed antibodies, and their infected state was ascertained later when the blood recipients were found to be infected, and the donors were traced. These transmissions reflect a failure of the system to provide test sites rather than a failure of the antibody test.

8. D. P. Francis and J. Chin, "The Prevention of Acquired Immunodeficiency Syndrome in the United States: An Objective Strategy for Medicine, Public Health, Business, and Community," *Journal of the American Medical Association*, vol. 257 (March 1987), pp. 1357–66.

among health care workers worldwide in fewer than 10 cases, and the maximum estimate of risk to health care workers with such exposure is 3 per 1,000 person-years. This is 30 times to 100 times less than the frequency of transmission of hepatitis B; indeed a study in San Francisco showed that health care workers exposed by accidental needle punctures to patients with documented hepatitis B, herpes, and HIV infections acquired the former two infections at significant rates but failed to become infected with HIV.[9] In health care settings, "universal precautions" should prevail, that is, based on the assumption that everyone may be infected with HIV, hepatitis B, or another potentially infectious agent, all patients should be treated with the same precautions. HIV, however, is far less readily transmitted than are many other viruses and bacteria that pose potential risks.

There is no instance in which a health care worker has transmitted HIV to a recipient of care.

Finally, mosquitoes and other biting insects have been shown not to transmit HIV.[10]

Once the virus is transmitted, antibodies detectable by standard tests appear uniformly within six to twelve weeks; exceptions are rare. Once the antibody response develops, it is sustained until well into the course of clinical AIDS, when it occasionally disappears.[11]

After an asymptomatic interval marked only by the sustained presence of antibody (and virus in blood, semen, and cervical secretions) infected persons begin to develop signs and symptoms of HIV infection,

9. T. L. Kuhls and others, "Occupational Risk of HIV, HBV, and HSV-2 Infections in Health Care Personnel Caring for AIDS Patients," *American Journal of Public Health*, vol. 77 (October 1987), pp. 1306–09.

10. L. Miike, *Do Insects Transmit AIDS?*, United States Congress, Office of Technology Assessment Health Program (Government Printing Office, 1987).

11. A much publicized report from Finland suggested that delays of many months before the antibody appeared occurred with significant frequency. This report contradicts extensive data gathered in many other clinical centers and is currently thought perhaps to reflect technical problems with the study; efforts to validate or amend the conclusions are under way. A. Ranki and others, "Long Latency Precedes Overt Seroconversion in Sexually Transmitted Human-Immunodeficiency-Virus Infection," *Lancet*, September 12, 1987, pp. 589–93.

progressing to AIDS. Development of at least some HIV-related symptoms has occurred in over 75 percent of persons known to have been infected for at least five years;[12] and it is feared that longer study will ultimately yield an even higher percentage. The current estimate of average interval from onset of infection to diagnosis of AIDS is seven years, with a range estimated to extend to fifteen years.[13] Thus the vast majority of HIV-infected persons will test positive in screening programs several years before illness (if indeed they ever become ill at all).

The diseases caused by HIV infection were initially diagnosed variously as the lymphadenopathy syndrome, AIDS-related complex, and AIDS. These categories were of necessity kept separate early in the epidemic despite widely held suspicion that they represented stages of the same underlying disease. The advent of diagnostic techniques for HIV infection, notably the antibody tests and virus cultivation in tissue culture, facilitated a rational understanding of these categories of disease. It is now evident that all those conditions are simply variations and gradations of severity of the effects of the human immunodeficiency virus. AIDS represents the final and most serious aspect of the infection, although an individual patient may progress to lethal illness without ever having the specific manifestations that are required to fit the official definition of AIDS.

The prognosis of AIDS is uniformly dismal. The life expectancy after diagnosis rarely exceeds two years. The new antiviral agent AZT, licensed by the Food and Drug Administration in 1987, has been shown effective in prolonging life and restoring some improved health to those patients who can tolerate its considerable toxic side effects, which usually include marked bone marrow suppression resulting in a dependence on intermittent blood transfusion; but the palliation is not durable and ultimately progression of the disease occurs. Thus it remains true that AIDS is one of the most deadly illnesses of man.[14]

12. W. Lang and others, "Clinical, Immunologic, and Serologic Findings in Men at Risk for Acquired Immunodeficiency Syndrome: The San Francisco Men's Health Study," *Journal of the American Medical Association*, vol. 257 (January 1987), pp. 326–30.

13. J. W. Curran and others, "Epidemiology of HIV Infection and AIDS in the United States," *Science*, vol. 239 (February 1988), pp. 610–16.

THE HIV ANTIBODY TEST AND PUBLIC HEALTH PROGRAMS

The cardinal goal of public health programs in the AIDS epidemic is to curtail further spread of the virus. Since transmission is limited to sexual and drug-using behaviors that are (by definition) private and consensual in nature, education through counseling of infected individuals and those whose behavior puts them at high risk of becoming infected is the most powerful available weapon of containment. Vaccines for HIV are likely to take more than a decade to develop, if indeed they prove feasible at all. Curative therapies are unlikely ever to be devised, given the intimacy with which the viral genome inserts itself into cellular DNA at the outset of infection. Drug treatments such as AZT will surely advance, but they will be palliative and their cost will surely remain prohibitive.

Given these facts, screening programs for HIV must be critically assessed for their potential contribution to containment of the epidemic. Positive contributions of testing will be in the context of individual counseling and education about risk behavior and means of spread.[15] It is difficult to imagine conditions where such personal counseling related to individual risk could be as effective when testing was mandatory as when it had been done in a voluntary setting.

The efficacy of counseling and education in the context of voluntary testing programs is currently under study in many locales. While initial

14. J. E. Osborn, "The AIDS Epidemic: Six Years," *Annual Review of Public Health,* vol. 9 (January 1988), pp. 551–83.

15. Counseling of individuals with high risk behavior is important whether the test is positive or negative. It is not uncommon for persons testing negative to assume, from their good luck to date, that they are somehow immune and will continue to lead a charmed life in the face of further risk. It is obvious that seropositive individuals must be counseled to protect others, but it is also crucial to convey the full range of information about the meaning of being infected with HIV, including the likelihood that years of good health may still be ahead; for suicide is a frequent occurrence in the wake of being told about seropositivity—even more frequent than after diagnoses of AIDS or of cancer.

expectations of absolute or radical behavior change were disappointed, there are increasing numbers of data sets that substantiate the effectiveness of education in achieving significant behavior modification and resultant risk reduction. In one recent study of a group of gay men with entrenched patterns of high risk sexual behavior,[16] individuals who knew of their positive antibody status showed a marked decrement in risky behavior and significantly increased use of condoms. Most strikingly, in a defined group of gay men in San Francisco who had earlier converted from no HIV antibodies to testing positive for HIV (seroconversion) at a rate of several percent a year, not a single seroconversion occurred in 1987. Similarly, the yearly rate of seroconversion among gay men in New York City—which earlier was at or above 5 percent a year—dropped below 1 percent in 1987. These experiences and data reinforce the desirability of an approach that optimizes the chance for behavior change through education for prevention as the most hopeful route to public health control of HIV.

The potential for voluntary testing to curtail the U.S. epidemic is nearly unique. Nevertheless, serious impediments exist to participation in testing programs by persons with high risk behavior. Most of the stumbling blocks stem directly or indirectly from the consequences of irrational and misplaced public fear of contagion. Because of the lack of a national education program about HIV and AIDS, public anxiety has far outstripped reality: the perception that a person is infected, or related to someone who is infected, or even merely a member of a "high risk group" can and does lead to extraordinary depredations of living circumstances and civil liberties.

This public terror and misinformation highlight the elements that are essential to the achievement of a successful program of widespread voluntary testing:

—Informed consent must be obtained before testing proceeds.[17]

16. J. L. Martin, "The Impact of AIDS on Gay Male Sexual Behavior Patterns in New York City," *American Journal of Public Health*, vol. 77 (May 1987), pp. 578–81.

17. In the blood donor screening program, a person is informed of the right *not to donate*. Once a donor has decided to proceed, he or she is counseled before donation. Afterward the donor is given no choice about whether to be told

—Counseling is the key component in the process and should be done both before and after the test.[18]

—Ready availability of testing is important since the decision to be tested is likely to be a difficult one for persons with established patterns of high risk behavior. It is distressing to note that the waiting period in California in 1987 was nine weeks. Additionally, testing locale can be important as a determinant in a person's decision to seek testing. If the only available site is the sexually transmitted diseases clinic or a forbidding inner city locale, it can be a big disincentive to persons with closeted risk behavior.

—The cost of the test should be reasonable. The basic cost of the screening test most commonly used can be as low as $2 to $5 per test. And yet currently, couples in Illinois who wish to marry, and are required as of January 1, 1988, to have been HIV tested, are being charged $50 to $70 per person. The rate of application for marriage licenses in Illinois has dropped drastically since the new policy was enacted. As the epidemic advances into the economically disadvantaged "underclass" of American society, cost may well become critical to voluntary participation in testing programs for many persons at high risk.

—Reliability is another key consideration. The HIV screening ELISA test is as accurate and reliable as any test in the medical armamentarium. Nevertheless, false positives will occur; and under these circumstances, repeat ELISA testing and another test—usually the Western Blot—are required to establish the meaning and significance of the initial positive result. The Western Blot test is subject to great variability depending on the testing laboratory, as was carefully discussed by Larry Miike in congressional testimony last fall. [19]

---

the result of the test. It is not permissible to withhold the results once they are obtained, regardless of the donor's wishes.

18. When present programs are evaluated for efficacy there should be a caveat about counseling because it is often cursory and brief. For instance, in the state of Virginia, which has the best record of counseling effort to date, the average counseling interval per individual tested is only 9.5 minutes.

19. L. Miike, *AIDS Antibody Testing,* Hearings before the House Committee on Small Business, Subcommittee on Regulation and Business Opportunities, 100 Cong. 1 sess. (GPO, 1987).

Clearly premature notification is possible in the interim between initial and subsequent tests. These matters require careful attention to avoid traumatizing an uninfected individual with information that might later require retraction.

A few exceptional circumstances may warrant consideration of mandatory testing. The criterion to be used in judging such proposed exceptions should be the identification of a clear-cut, demonstrable need to know for public health reasons. Examples would perhaps include homosexual rape in prison or very unusual circumstances such as the biting of a pregnant police officer by the person she had arrested.

Possibly, some elective surgery might warrant involuntary testing although "universal precautions" should be more than sufficient to provide protection in the health care workplace. Whenever such involuntary testing is deployed, certain safeguards should be ensured;[20] subjects to be tested should be informed that testing is to be done and should be given the results, with careful pre- and post-test counseling. Due process should be scrupulously observed.

Circumstances that could contribute to an individual's decision to undergo testing would include contemplation of marriage or establishment of permanent relationships, pregnancy, the possibility of AZT prophylaxis if infected (the efficacy of AZT in delaying the onset of clinical signs and symptoms of HIV infection is currently under experimental test), the possible hazard of other therapies (for example, high dose steroids) if infected, and a wish to order life priorities.

The major reasons for refraining from participation are fear of learning the result and fear of discrimination in many areas including health insurance, employment, housing, dental care, and school. Acts of public violence such as arson have occurred against persons known or thought to be HIV positive.

Finally, the balance of considerations could change greatly if treatment or vaccine options improved—but as noted earlier, such changes are unlikely within the next decade. Facets of the picture that could be improved almost immediately, however, include public information— which would diminish the element of fear in the equation—and

20. R. Bayer, C. Levine, and S. M. Wolf, "HIV Antibody Screening. An Ethical Framework for Evaluating Proposed Programs," *Journal of the American Medical Association*, vol. 256 (October 1986), pp. 1768–74.

nondiscrimination legislation that could protect participants from social reprisal.[21]

COMPARISONS BETWEEN ISSUES OF AIDS TESTING AND DRUG TESTING

Some similarity exists between AIDS testing and drug testing. Both involve technologies that are well-developed and acceptably accurate, although false positives are problems, especially in low risk populations where they may greatly outnumber true positives.

The rationale for testing in each case is driven by third-party involvement, specifically by issues of public safety. Thus the testing of airline pilots for substance abuse raises little concern, whereas similar testing of an office worker might be more problematic. In HIV testing, the usual public perception of the safety issue stems from ignorance of transmission data; only in the "sex industry" do workplace issues of safety arise.[22]

Given that both HIV testing and drug testing have, as a fundamental goal, behavior change on the part of the tested individual, they are subject to similar distortions. In recent antidrug "crusades," emotionalism and moralism have threatened the success of testing programs. The need for voluntary participation and informed behavior change by individuals at high risk of contracting AIDS makes it likely that these negative attitudes can compromise those programs as well. Indeed, a recent study revealed that self-described homophobic attitudes were a significant negative component in physicians' delivery of medical care

21. The usefulness of such nondiscrimination legislation (as exemplified by the Waxman bill) is unarguable, but it seems to be a politically untouchable issue and is likely to die for lack of congressional support.

22. Recently some concern has arisen about the possibility that incipient neurologic disease might jeopardize performance in some situations. This will be an issue difficult to debate rationally, since it may be greatly overdrawn by groups intent on finding a rationale for identification and "quarantine" of HIV-positive individuals. Because of the importance of these issues, a World Health Organization Consultation on the neuropsychiatric aspects of HIV infection was convened in Geneva in March 1988 to work on the development of policy related to this feature of HIV infection.

to homosexual patients;[23] and intravenous drug users are widely considered "beyond the pale." Clearly such attitudes can deter many persons whose behavior constitutes the key to further HIV spread or its containment from participating in voluntary testing programs.

Finally, one flaw is common to both drug testing and HIV testing. In drug testing the true intent is containment of substance abuse, and yet testing for alcohol abuse is almost never included in the battery of tests employed. With HIV, the perception of groups at risk has led to a potentially serious problem. The high risk behavior of bisexual men or intermittent intravenous drug users may be entirely missed. In both drug and AIDS testing, focus on a positive or negative test result rather than on behavior counteracts the effectiveness of testing.

THE CONNECTION BETWEEN THE AIDS AND DRUG EPIDEMICS

Analysts note that drug use is the key pathway to the broadening of the AIDS epidemic in the United States. As noted earlier, HIV infection rates among intravenous drug users vary greatly from one city to another. In New York and New Jersey rates of 60 percent to 80 percent prevalence of HIV antibody among addicts have prevailed in the past year or more. In the past two years most persons with AIDS admitted to New York hospitals have acquired their HIV infection through intravenous drug use. This complicates care, contributes to a higher frequency and longer duration of hospitalization, and markedly increases health care costs, when contrasted with San Francisco, for example, where less than 3 percent of AIDS cases thus far have occurred in persons whose sole risk factor was intravenous drug use.

Pediatric AIDS is a direct or indirect consequence of intravenous drug use in over 90 percent of U.S. cases. While the number of pediatric cases to date has been a small part of the overall magnitude of the epidemic, a comprehensive survey of newborn babies born in New York city in late 1987 revealed that one out of every sixty-one infants had antibodies to HIV. This figure raised public alarm and surprise when it was reported, and yet it confirms almost exactly the findings one to two years earlier

23. C. E. Lewis, H. E. Freeman, and C. R. Corey, "AIDS-Related Competence of California's Primary Care Physicians," *American Journal of Public Health*, vol. 77 (July 1987), pp. 795–99.

obtained by the U.S. military services in their program of screening volunteers for HIV antibodies. They found a national rate of seropositivity of 1.6 per 1,000 among men and 0.6 per 1,000 among women; but in the New York City area the rates were much higher and nearly equal between the sexes: 1.6 per 100 men and 1.3 per 100 women. The sources of infection in these persons are not easily established (since the military rejects HIV-positive volunteers without counseling), but it is likely that both intravenous drug use and heterosexual intercourse contributed significantly to this demographic pattern of seropositivity, which presages a substantial shift in future AIDS cases.

In view of the manifest importance of intravenous drug use to the HIV epidemic, it is startling to note that little has been done to attack the connection between AIDS and drugs directly. Even efforts to ensure access to clean needles have been frustrated or complicated by moralistic protests against "seeming to condone" intravenous drug use. Yet treatment facilities and options available to addicts were greatly overtaxed even before HIV gave impetus to the wish to curtail intravenous drug use. New York City, with an estimated 200,000 heroin addicts, had less than 25,000 treatment slots as of 1986, and that number had not increased since the early 1970s. Drug addicts who seek treatment are relegated to waiting lists several months long; and yet the needle issue is unresolved and addicts continue at high risk of spreading or contracting the virus, as do their sexual partners. The need for effective, pragmatic revisions of public policies in this area is strikingly apparent.

Private Sector Concerns

AIDS has quickly become one of the most publicized diseases of our time—and with good reason: this tragic disease has now assumed global dimensions, placing increasing demands on the resources of all areas of society—federal, state, and local governments, as well as the private sector. The personal tragedies and liabilities resulting from AIDS underscore the need for a consensus on how to respond to the attendant economic problems for individuals and for society.

Similarly, the widespread abuse of illegal drugs has gained the attention of the nation. This concern was heightened by the media attention and public alarm that followed the Amtrak train crash on January 4, 1987, in Maryland. Tests showed the presence of marijuana in the systems of the brakeman and engineer. As the incidence and prevalence of drug abuse in the United States have risen, many employers have developed pre-employment and in-service drug screening programs to ensure the safe and productive conduct of their businesses.

Many issues surround the private sector's use of AIDS and drug tests. In response to grim projections of AIDS cases increasing at an alarming rate, the insurance industry seeks to use the best and most current medical test available to evaluate the risk of AIDS, just as it evaluates the risk of any other illness. In response to the escalating problem of substance abuse in the workplace and increasing evidence on the debilitating effects that drugs have on performance, employers seek to evaluate applicants and employees to ensure a drug-free workplace.

Private sector concerns were reviewed by panelists Russel Iuculano, senior counsel, American Council of Life Insurance; Phillip Shellhaas, program director, IBM Corporation; and Peggy Taylor, deputy director, legislative department, AFL-CIO.

AIDS TESTING BY INSURERS

As of February 1, 1988, more than 52,000 Americans were diagnosed as having AIDS. The cumulative total of deaths now exceeds 29,000, more than half of those afflicted.[1] It is conservatively estimated that as many as 270,000 Americans may contract this invariably fatal disease by 1991.[2]

The epidemic raises difficult and controversial public policy questions, especially questions of who shall bear the enormous health care costs associated with this disease and how to allocate these costs in a fair, equitable, and fiscally prudent manner. A widely quoted estimate of the cost of care for AIDS patients projects a rise from $1.1 billion in 1986 to $8.5 billion in 1991.[3] A closely related issue is the extent to which life and health insurers will be permitted to take AIDS into account in underwriting insurance products. Specifically, should state legislators and insurance regulators prohibit life and health insurers from testing for infection by the AIDS virus?

In the face of mounting AIDS cases and frightening government projections for the future, life and health insurers have reason to be concerned about insuring those suffering from AIDS and persons infected with the AIDS virus (HIV virus). They are also concerned about the impact of current policyholders who may develop AIDS. Insurers will meet their commitments to those people and to the future victims of AIDS who are already insured. While maintaining their commitment to pay benefits for existing policyholders, insurance companies are anxious to insure new policyholders if they can be

1. See U. S. Centers for Disease Control, *AIDS Weekly Surveillance Report*, February 1, 1988 (Atlanta, Ga.: Centers for Disease Control, 1988).

2. U.S. Department of Health and Human Services, Public Health Service, "Public Service Plan for the Prevention and Control of AIDS and the AIDS Virus," report of the Coolfont Planning Conference, June 4–6, 1986, *Journal of the U. S. Public Health Service*, vol. 101 (July-August 1986), pp. 341–48.

3. A. A. Scitovsky and D. P. Rice, "Estimates of the Direct and Indirect Costs of Acquired Immunodeficiency Syndrome in the United States, 1985, 1986, and 1991," *Journal of the U. S. Public Health Service*, vol. 102 (July-August 1986), pp. 5–17.

properly classified as to the risk they represent. To classify applicants properly, life and health insurers must evaluate the risk of AIDS just as they evaluate diabetes, heart disease, cancer, or other medical conditions affecting health and life.

NATURE OF THE CONTROVERSY

Throughout history, life and health insurers have been able to use all relevant, reliable, and effective predictors of risk to underwrite and price their policies fairly. Traditionally, insurers have been allowed to condition their offer to contract on acceptable results of medical tests, in recognition of the insurer's right to know as much about the applicant's health as necessary to fully consider the risk.

The spread of AIDS, however, has seriously challenged this right. Perhaps at no other time have state legislators, insurance regulators, special interest groups, and the media expressed such intensity of interest in the process by which insurers underwrite policies and classify risk.

To some extent, concerns about discrimination against homosexuals have fueled legislative and regulatory challenges. By its nature, risk classification means the identification of risk and classification of individuals. Until the company understands the risk, it cannot know whether, or on what basis, to insure the risk. The controversy stems f●m the fact that homosexual males, constituting 63.6 percent of the AIDS cases to date, are the group at greatest risk.[4] Therefore, persons who are at risk for AIDS but do not have the disease fear the denial of coverage based solely on irrelevant lifestyle, sexual orientation, or other inferential information that may be gathered during the application process.

The life and health insurance industry shares the concern that sexual orientation not be an allowable determinant in making insurance judgments. During 1986, the industry worked with insurance regulators and gay rights leaders to devise national standards that bar consideration of sexual orientation in insurance underwriting. The guidelines were adopted by the National Association of Insurance Commissioners

4. See Centers for Disease Control, *AIDS Weekly Surveillance Report*, p. 3, note 1.

(NAIC) in December 1986.[5] Colorado, Delaware, Florida, Oregon, South Dakota, Texas, and Wisconsin have already adopted regulations patterned after the NAIC model guidelines.

Some people are also concerned about the insurance industry's ability to successfully protect AIDS-related medical information. They fear discrimination against infected individuals in employment, housing, or other areas if knowledge of the infection becomes known.

Some public policymakers easily subordinate risk classification when it is examined in relation to perceived civil or social rights. The rush to ensure "fairness" for persons at risk for AIDS has resulted in a great deal of proposed legislation. In at least three jurisdictions laws have been enacted to prohibit the use of AIDS-related testing for insurance purposes. Those laws mandate the abandonment of time-honored and sensible risk classification principles.[6]

RISK CLASSIFICATION FOR AIDS

If people knew exactly how long they were going to live or when they were going to be ill and need medical care, they could plan their finances accordingly and would hardly need life or health insurance. But because the future is unknown to most people, they purchase insurance for financial protection against unforeseen and unpredictable losses.

To price insurance fairly and equitably, insurance companies must know more about the applicant than the current state of that person's health. Insurers must be able to evaluate the chances of early death or future illness. That is why insurers ask questions about such things as smoking habits. Smokers usually pay higher premiums because their risk of developing cancer or heart disease is greater than that of nonsmokers. For the same reason, insurers believe it is imperative to ask relevant questions about the presence of the AIDS virus, and when appropriate, test for infection by the AIDS virus.

5. Advisory Committee on AIDS, "Medical-Lifestyle Questions and Underwriting Guidelines" (Kansas City, Mo., National Association of Insurance Commissioners, 1986).

6. See Calif. Health and Safety Code 199.21 (f) (West Supp. 1986) (effective April 4, 1985); D.C. Code Ann. 35-221 to 35-229 (Supp. 1987); and Wis. Stat. Ann. 631.90 (West Supp. 1986) (effective November 23, 1985).

Life and health insurers contend that laws that arbitrarily limit the use of medical information allow persons infected with the AIDS virus to obtain insurance at a price that does not truly reflect the risk they represent, resulting in their subsidy by low-risk policyholders. The subsidy is not only unfair to healthy, low-risk policyholders but also to life or health insurance applicants with other diseases.

Therefore, the essence of the life and health insurance industry's position is that AIDS must be treated for all insurance purposes as any other life-threatening illness.

VALIDITY OF AIDS ANTIBODY TESTS AS UNDERWRITING TOOLS

Medical authorities now generally believe that the protocol of body fluid tests known as the ELISA-ELISA-Western Blot (WB) series is highly accurate for determining the presence of infection with the HIV virus. The insurance industry administers this protocol of tests rather than a single test to identify HIV-infected applicants.

Once an individual is reliably identified as infected with the HIV virus, the U.S. Centers for Disease Control (CDC) estimates conservatively that such an individual's likelihood of contracting AIDS within five years can be estimated at 20 percent to 30 percent.[7] More recent studies have estimated the risk as high as 50 percent within ten years.[8]

No person unequivocally diagnosed as having AIDS has ever recovered.[9] Most victims die within two to three years of the appearance of the disease.[10]

The actuarial significance of these facts is difficult for insurers to ignore. Using the most conservative CDC estimate, 20 percent, 200 out of each 1,000 applicants testing positive on the ELISA-ELISA-WB series

7. U. S. Department of Health and Human Services, "Public Service Plan," p. 5.

8. National Academy of Sciences, Institute of Medicine, *Confronting AIDS: Directions for Public Health, Health Care and Research* (Washington, D. C.: National Academy Press, 1986).

9. National Institutes of Health, "The Acquired Immunodeficiency Syndrome: An Update," *Annals of Internal Medicine,* vol. 102 (January-June 1985), pp. 800, 802.

10. National Academy of Sciences, *Confronting AIDS,* p. 7.

will develop AIDS within five years and die within seven years. By contrast, life insurance mortality tables estimate that of a standard group of 1,000 persons aged 34, only 7.5 will die within seven years from all causes.[11] In other words, a seropositive (HIV-positive) applicant is twenty-six times more likely to die within seven years than a noninfected person, all other factors being equal. By comparison, a smoker is only twice as likely to die within seven years, a diabetic is four times more likely, and a prior heart attack victim five times more likely.

OPPOSITION TO TESTING

Jeffrey Levi of the National Gay and Lesbian Task Force stated at the October 27 conference that his organization's primary concern has been to maintain access to health insurance. While conceding the social consequences of being tested, he argued that the issue should be posed as one of denial of access to quality health care because of the desire by the health insurance industry to deny coverage to those who test positive for HIV infection. Moreover, Levi opined that the economic arguments for testing were more convincing in life insurance than they were for health insurance. Levi contended that no safety net existed for people who are denied health insurance, other than medicaid. He also called for the establishment of health insurance risk sharing pools for people who are uninsurable.

Finally, Levi argued that private health insurance is not just a business. It is a "social utility" that serves a social function to guarantee Americans access to adequate health care. Screening for AIDS results in the industry's avoidance of the AIDS risk rather than serving its social function.

AVAILABILITY OF HEALTH INSURANCE

In response to the issues raised by Levi, one must understand the limits on what the private health insurance industry can do and the role the

11. See Society of Actuaries, *Transactions: 1982 Reports of Mortality and Morbidity Experience* (Schaumburg, Ill.: Society of Actuaries, 1985), p. 55.

private sector plays in financing this country's medical bill. At last count, some 158 million Americans under the age of 65 were covered by some form of group health insurance, and 9 million more were covered solely by individual health insurance.[12] About 90 percent of the insured population is covered by group health insurance and 10 percent by individual insurance.[13] Thus most of the insured population is already covered by health insurance that will pay for AIDS-related medical care. Moreover, because most private health insurance is written as group, persons infected with HIV who are employable continue to maintain access to coverage despite their infected status. Group insurance does not usually involve the underwriting (or screening for HIV) of individuals within the group.

Group health insurance is not individually underwritten because if the group is large enough, the costs of the few who will experience substantial health care costs can be spread among the other employees in the group. Small groups, however, do not have enough people to spread the risk broadly enough to absorb the effect of adverse selection (that is, the tendency of persons to apply for insurance with knowledge that the insurer does not have, which leads an applicant to expect that the benefits he or she will receive are likely to exceed the premiums paid). For example, small employers may not decide to obtain coverage for their workers until a key employee or family member becomes aware that he or she will be incurring large medical expenses. To protect against adverse selection, insurers of small groups ask employees and covered dependents to submit information about their health to determine their insurability. This information may include testing for the presence of HIV antibodies. Small group health policies constitute about 7 percent of the group health insurance market.[14]

In Levi's view, health insurance is a social utility, but the industry believes that however important and valuable private health insurance is, it is not an entitlement. Private health insurance cannot solve all our

12. These are unpublished data from a 1986 survey by the Health Insurance Association of America, Washington, D.C., Thomas D. Musco, director of statistics.

13. Health Insurance Association of America, "Source Book of Health Insurance Data: 1986 Update" (Washington, D.C., HIAA, 1986).

14. HIAA 1986 survey.

social health care needs. It is no solution to a national health care crisis to deny health insurers the right to obtain the facts about the health of persons who apply for insurance. What public purpose would be served by allowing those individuals likely to develop AIDS health insurance at standard rates while other consumers pay higher premiums or are declined coverage because of serious health conditions other than AIDS? Barring HIV testing would merely shift the cost of AIDS from society at large to the health-insured population—a segment least able to bear the added cost. It could create a tremendous incentive for insurers selling individual and small group health insurance policies to consider whether they should continue offering such coverage rather than be forced to sell the policies on an unprofitable basis and jeopardize their solvency.

The private health insurance industry shares Levi's concern with the problems of uninsurable people in this country and agrees that states should be encouraged to establish pools for them. Fifteen states— Connecticut, Florida, Illinois, Indiana, Iowa, Maine, Minnesota, Montana, Nebraska, New Mexico, North Dakota, Oregon, Tennessee, Washington, and Wisconsin—have enacted such programs. All of the risk sharing pools already adopted have been for all uninsurable people, not just those infected with HIV. Usually, premiums are charged that are 150 percent of the average premium for comparable individual health insurance.

The industry disagrees with Levi about the appropriate source of financing for such pools. Most states that have enacted risk sharing pools fund them by assessments on insurers (based on their share of business in the state) with offsets against premium taxes for the amount of the assessment. Only Illinois offers direct general revenue financing by appropriating funds for pool assessments.[15] When states provide tax offsets, they are recognizing that responsibility for funding the losses that state pools often sustain must be broadly based and equitably apportioned. Controversy has developed because public policymakers seem more and more reluctant to impose new fiscal burdens on their governmental budgets. They are reluctant to commit state revenues or raise taxes to fund pools. Indeed, Minnesota repealed its premium tax offset.[16] Therefore, it becomes politically expedient to lay the socio-

15. Ill. Stat. Ann. chap. 73, pars. 1301–1314 (Smith-Hurd 1987).
16. Minn. Stat. Ann. 62E .01–.16 (West 1986).

medical-economic problem of uninsurable people at the feet of the insurance business. When the industry balks at pooling proposals that call for financing without assistance from general revenues, it is perceived precisely as stated by Levi—as an industry seeking to "wash its hands of the AIDS problem."

Another difficulty in financing these pools is section 514 of ERISA, which limits a state's ability to require self-insured employers to participate in such pools.[17] As more employers self-insure their employee benefit plans, there are fewer insured plans to assume the responsibility for the uninsurable population and hence participate in state pools. Consequently, the industry is concerned about its increasing financial responsibility as the premium base against which the pool's losses will be assessed shrinks.

To overcome the ERISA barrier to universal participation and to ensure that the social responsibility of providing coverage to the uninsurable population is fairly apportioned, the health insurance industry supports federal legislation to encourage states to establish state pools for otherwise uninsurable Americans. State-established pools should be funded through general revenue or any other broad-based mechanism that does not assign losses disproportionately to any segment of the population or corporate entity. Acceptable approaches include assessments against insurers with a premium tax offset or assessments against all employers with offsets against state income or employment taxes.

These approaches are far more preferable than requiring health insurers to abandon the principles on which private insurance is founded by expecting them to operate without taking AIDS into account in underwriting and pricing insurance.

DRUG TESTING IN THE WORKPLACE

Because of the widespread use of illegal drugs, an increasing number of employers are implementing drug detection programs in pre-employment exams and for in-service employees. Employers are concerned for the health, welfare, and safety of their employees. They want to protect private property and preserve a productive working environment. They

17. 29 U. S. C. 1101–1462 (1982).

are also concerned about the safety of the public. While employees support the goal of keeping drugs out of the workplace, they fear that the rush by employers to adopt drug detection programs may invade privacy, subject them to harassment if used on a random basis, and adversely affect employee morale. Nevertheless, neither employers nor employees want state and federal legislators to enact legislation governing drug testing in the workplace without giving the matter a great deal of deliberation and thought.

Phillip Shellhaas, program director of the IBM corporation, explained his company's position on drug abuse and why IBM has chosen to do a limited amount of drug testing to ensure a safe and healthy workplace. Shellhaas stressed IBM's longstanding commitment to maintaining the confidentiality of information about employees. Before embarking on drug testing, the company developed policies to balance the concern over what would be done with information, why it would be collected, and how confidentiality would be maintained.

DRUG SCREENING IN THE PRE-EMPLOYMENT EXAM

Shellhaas reported that IBM makes the use of drugs a consideration in hiring. All applicants are asked to take a drug screening as part of the pre-employment process. IBM clearly informs job applicants that drug screening is a required part of the pre-employment examination and that a positive drug finding means that no formal job offer will be made.

IBM explains any positive test results to the applicant. The company informs the applicant that he or she may reapply in six months and be reconsidered with a blank slate. The applicant is also allowed to explain why he or she might have failed the test result, for example, an applicant might be taking medication that adversely affects the test result.

Peggy Taylor, deputy director of the legislative department of the AFL-CIO, did not take issue with the use of drug tests in the hiring process. She did express concern that employers use reliable tests and that employers use laboratories qualified to provide accurate test results. Shellhaas responded that to ensure accuracy, all positive findings to the initial urinalysis are confirmed by a second test. In addition, the company takes great care to select the best scientific technology.

TESTING OF IN-SERVICE EMPLOYEES

Shellhaas explained IBM's use of testing in-service employees as based on the identification of a problem that is performance related. A test would only be called for when a noticeable, definable degradation in performance occurs that is unexplainable by other factors, thus triggering suspicion of drug use. The medical department makes a final determination about whether a test should be applied. The test is done as a "constructive confrontation" to avoid the denial typical of drug users. The test is used as a final resort when encouragement of the employee to confront his or her problem through voluntary employee assistance has not been successful. Shellhaas noted that IBM's decision for testing employees based on "reasonable suspicion" had been corroborated by several state legislatures. The definition of reasonable suspicion has been restricted in some instances to cases in which the employee is "under the influence" or "impaired" on the job.[18]

A critical issue to unions is a definition of what circumstances trigger a test. Taylor opined that most employee groups would not object to testing on reasonable suspicion of drug use, based on measurable work impairment. She disagreed with the notion of potential impairment on the job, because of its hypothetical nature. She believes it is more appropriate for employers to be concerned about actual measure of work impairment.

Taylor stressed the need for clear legislative guidelines on the circumstances of drug testing. She also outlined the importance of legislation that limits the discretion of supervisors to ensure equitable treatment of employees. The legislation should articulate what is reasonable suspicion. Another area needing legislative standards is post-accident testing. No objection was made to the need for testing

18. See, for example, 1987 Conn. Laws Public Act 87-551 (effective October 1, 1987); 1987 Iowa Laws chap. 208 (effective July 1, 1987); 1987 Minnesota Laws chap. 388 (effective September 1, 1987); and 1987 Vermont Laws Act 61 (effective September 1, 1987).

after on-the-job accidents that may indicate impaired performance so long as qualifying incidents are clearly defined in advance. Such incidents should be truly significant in the particular workplace.

Taylor characterized random drug testing as the most egregious kind of testing to any employee and union group in light of the potential for harassment of selected employees that the employer doesn't like. To prove that the concern was more than hypothetical, Taylor cited an incident in which an employer in a plant in Maine tested seven out of ten employees; the first seven out of ten tested were on a collective bargaining committee.

Lee Dogoloff from the American Council for Drug Education suggested that in certain circumstances, when the performance of employees directly affects the safety of the public and other employees, random or anticipatory testing is appropriate. He cited, for example, the rights of children to be protected from a bus driver under the influence of marijuana and the rights of a construction worker to be protected from a crane operator suffering from similar effects.

In response to the example of the crane operator, Taylor suggested that the trained supervisor could discern signs of drug use and prevent the operator from getting into the crane cab. Then the employer would have reasonable suspicion for testing. Taylor questioned whether random testing would identify every impaired crane operator before he gets into the cab. She recommended that the small sampling of drug users identified be weighed against the impact of random testing on the work force. In her view, the theory behind random testing is one of intimidation that could seriously debilitate the morale of the work force. Taylor also noted the extreme difficulty of defining safety-sensitive positions. Although certain occupations such as airline pilots are obviously safety sensitive, it is unclear where to draw the line as responsibility decreases.

Peter Heseltine from the University of Southern California also questioned the effectiveness of random testing, as well as the assumptions on which it is based. In his opinion, random testing incorrectly assumes the use of drugs is a random event in a group of workers. Without evidence that the use of drugs is a random event among workers, the use of random testing is inappropriate. Therefore, to detect individuals who were drug users, employers would have to test every day under current technology. The resulting intrusion and cost become overwhelming.

Shellhaas, while noting that IBM did not conduct random drug tests, disagreed with Taylor about the tests. He believes that in certain occupations random testing is appropriate. Certain employees responsible for public safety, fiduciary matters, or carrying liability can simply understand in advance that the job will require drug screening. They should not expect privacy—much as people now expect to take physical exams in order to qualify for certain occupations or activities.

Besides concern about the circumstances that trigger a test, the AFL-CIO is focusing on the procedural protections of whatever testing is done. Taylor recommended fully informing employees of all the procedures under the testing programs so they know what to expect, what their rights are, what they are going to be tested for, and what levels are considered positive or negative. The union also advises furnishing the employee with sufficient information to exercise his right to contest the test result.

REHABILITATION AND EDUCATION

Unions want to make sure that employees found chemically dependent are given the chance to be rehabilitated rather than summarily dismissed. Thus the AFL-CIO supports legislation requiring employers who use mandatory drug test programs to establish and maintain rehabilitation programs.

IBM is among the employers who have installed an Employee Assistance Program (EAP) designed to give counseling and professional help to chemically dependent employees. The EAP is free, voluntary, and confidential. Employees who voluntarily request assistance for drug or alcohol problems are given assistance in arranging for a rehabilitation program, and IBM reimburses most of their expenses. IBM has made the cost of outpatient drug and alcohol treatment reimbursable under its employee medical plan.

To support rehabilitation efforts and confront the drug abuse problem, IBM emphasizes education programs aimed at preventing drug problems from developing. Its active education program includes articles written in employee magazines, distributed broadly to all employees. These programs also make it clear that IBM will not tolerate drug use at any time.

S. 1041

Taylor cited federal legislation S. 1041, which illustrates the complexities connected with legislation that supports drug testing in the workplace. The bill was introduced in response to the public alarm about safety in the transportation area and the need to eliminate the use of illegal drugs by individuals operating or helping to operate aircraft, railroads, trucks, and buses. As reported out of the Senate Committee on Commerce, Science, and Transportation, the bill would establish drug and alcohol testing programs for certain individuals employed in safety-sensitive positions in the aviation, rail, bus, and truck industries. It would require five types of testing, including pre-employment, post-accident, random, periodic recurring, and on reasonable suspicion.

Taylor expressed concern for the speed with which the bill was reported by the committee. She also criticized the bill for its lack of procedural protections, failure to require rehabilitation, and failure to address the issue of an employee's rights to appeal.

On October 29, 1987, the Senate passed an amendment to S. 1485 (the Air Passenger Protection Act of 1987) which incorporated the substance of S. 1041 but added more stringent protection of privacy and safeguards for laboratory testing to ensure validity and accuracy. The floor debate focused on the bill's controversial provisions for mandatory random testing. Senator John C. Danforth, Republican of Missouri, argued that eliminating drug usage by transportation employees in safety-sensitive positions required a strong deterrent, such as the threat of being detected and sanctioned for drug use. In his view, random testing was the "essential ingredient" of any drug testing program.[19] To support his opinion, he cited the testimony of Federal Railway Administrator John Riley for the proposition that testing for reasonable suspicion is not adequate to ensure that drug-related accidents do not occur. Riley testified that in the Maryland accident, the Conrail brakeman and engineer (who were found to have signs of marijuana in their systems) were in the presence of their supervisor immediately before the accident. Nevertheless, they were able to mask their behavior to prevent detection by their supervisor.[20]

19. *Congressional Record*, daily edition (October 29, 1987), p. S15433.
20. Ibid.

Opponents of random testing, led by Senator Daniel Inouye, Democrat of Hawaii, argued that the bill was unlikely to withstand constitutional scrutiny as a Fourth Amendment violation of an employee's right to privacy. They contended that the employees' constitutional right to privacy outweighed the government's interest in drug testing without reasonable suspicion.[21] Eventually, S. 1485 became incorporated into the omnibus drug bill passed by the Senate, but the provisions stemming from S. 1041 were dropped in conference.

AIDS TESTING IN THE WORKPLACE

Neither Shellhaas nor Taylor addressed the issue of screening employees for AIDS in great detail. Shellhaas reported that IBM had carefully considered the issues associated with employee testing and decided not to test at the present time. IBM has no particular interest in identifying persons infected with HIV with regard to their employment. The company allows such persons to work so long as they maintain the ability to do the job. Shellhaas said he believed that many companies had chosen a similar course of action.

IBM's decision not to request that applicants or employees submit to AIDS testing recognizes the wide variety of legal restraints that may circumscribe an employer's ability to act on the results of such a test. For example, California, Texas, and Wisconsin have already enacted laws prohibiting the testing of applicants for AIDS to determine suitability for employment.[22] Individuals with positive HIV test results may also be protected by federal and state statutes prohibiting discrimination based on handicap.

The principal federal statutory remedy available to persons objecting to employment-based screening is the Vocational Rehabilitation Act of 1973 (Rehabilitation Act).[23] The act prohibits federal contractors and recipients of federal financial assistance from discriminating in employment on the basis of handicap. Private sector employers, such as

21. Ibid., p. 15436.
22. See Calif. Health and Safety Code 199.21 (f) (West Supp. 1986) (effective April 4, 1985); Tex. Rev. Civ. Stat. Ann. art. 4419b-1, 9.02 (Vernon 1987) (effective September 1, 1987); and Wis. Stat. Ann. 103.15 et seq. (1986).
23. See 29 U. S. C. 781 et seq. (1986).

hospitals receiving medicare or medicaid payments or manufacturers doing business with the government, come within the scope of the act.

Section 504 of the Rehabilitation Act provides as follows:

No otherwise qualified individual with handicaps in the United States . . . shall, solely by reason of his handicap, be excluded from the participation in, be denied the benefits of, or be subjected to discrimination under any program or activity receiving federal financial assistance.[24]

The federal act defines a handicapped person as any person who "(i) has a physical or mental impairment which substantially limits one or more of such person's major life activities; (ii) has a record of such an impairment; or (iii) is regarded as having such an impairment."[25]

Under the terms of the federal act, an individual satisfying the definition of "handicapped" is protected so long as the individual is otherwise qualified to perform the job. The law also prohibits an employer from denying employment or terminating an employee if reasonable accommodation can be made without undue hardship to the employer to enable the handicapped person to perform the job.[26]

On October 13 and 14, 1987, more than 200 representatives from major companies met in Chicago at a conference entitled, "AIDS: Corporate America Responds." The conference (which was initiated by the Allstate Insurance Company) was concerned with AIDS in the workplace, and the attendees divided themselves into task forces to focus on areas of concern. One task force issued a report analyzing the legal issues connected with AIDS in the workplace.

Each federal and state court that has considered the question, notes the report, has held that AIDS is a handicap entitled to protection by federal and state laws prohibiting discrimination against handicapped individuals.[27] Since AIDS is a handicap protected by such laws, the

24. 29 U. S. C. 794 (1986).

25. 29 U. S. C. 706 (8) (B) (Supp. 1987).

26. 29 U. S. C. 794 (1986).

27. Allstate Insurance Co., *AIDS: Corporate America Responds* (Northbrook, Ill.: Allstate Insurance Co., 1988), pp. 44, 46, 47, citing *Shuttleworth* v. *Broward County*, 41 FEP Cases 406 (S. D. Fla. 1986); and *Cronin* v. *New England Telephone Company*, 41 FEP Cases 1273 (Mass. Sup. Jud. Ct. 1986).

report contends that testing for HIV is likely to be considered illegal because testing positive cannot be shown to be related to performance on the job.[28]

The report also stated that forty-seven states and the District of Columbia have laws prohibiting handicap discrimination with statutory language similar to the language in the federal act.[29] Many of these state laws not only protect persons who are actually impaired but also use the federal act's definition of "handicapped individual" to protect persons who are "regarded as having" an impairment.[30] The existence of this broader language is significant. State handicap laws that protect persons "regarded as having" a handicap could extend to an HIV-positive person if an employer excludes an otherwise qualified person from employment because the employer erroneously regards a positive test result as meaning that the individual has AIDS and its debilitating attributes.

The report illustrated the need for employers to become educated about all aspects of the law and to exercise caution if they are considering testing.

28. Ibid., p. 49.
29. Ibid., p. 48.
30. Ibid.

NORMAN E. ZINBERG, M.D.

Mandatory Testing for Drug Use and AIDS

When I first heard that a conference was to be held that would combine the two topics of AIDS and illicit drug use around the central rubric of mandatory testing, my response was negative. It seemed unreasonable to combine a disastrous health issue with a complex social-political issue whose public health aspects were minimal. But the more I considered mandatory testing, the harder I found it to differentiate between the two subjects and the more their similarities came to light. Then the overriding question became, What can the United States hope to accomplish by employing a coercive testing device that, even according to its proponents, overrides certain individual liberties? Those favoring mandatory testing hope to prevent both the spread of AIDS and the destructive consequences of drug abuse. With the first purpose, there can be no quarrel, and even with the second the quarrel is an old one: it has to do with what means justify what ends, and what is human vice as against what is a destructive disease. Many other questions also arise, including not only whether mandatory testing is the most effective way of accomplishing our goals but also whether hidden and unacknowledged in these efforts at so-called prevention there is not the attempt to achieve a kind of social, legal, and moral dominance over U.S. citizens.

The various attempts being made to control drug use and AIDS in our society point to two conflicting approaches to these problems.

The first concentrates on helping users to live their lives more safely,

The implications of mandatory testing for public policy were reviewed by panelists Norman Zinberg, M.D., Harvard University, Department of Psychiatry; Billy Jones, Whitman-Walker clinic; and Donald Ian Macdonald, special assistant to the president and director of the White House Drug Abuse Policy Office, Reagan administration. This paper reflects the views of Norman Zinberg.

while the second attacks the lifestyle that is associated with the destructive consequences of illicit drug use. The first approves of the use of condoms and explains how they can be used homosexually or heterosexually, while the second insists that all educational efforts should include pro-family messages—messages that directly oppose unmarried sex, abortion, and homosexuality. The first approach differentiates among drugs based on their addiction potential and teaches how to use them (or any other kind of intoxicant, such as alcohol) in a controlled, responsible manner, while the second considers all illicit drug use destructive and therefore makes no attempt to differentiate among drugs or between experimental use and abuse. The second approach treats both tobacco and alcohol with special deference, even while mentioning that they may be dangerous. It also opposes any relaxation of the "Just Say No" approach to illicit drug use, no matter how practical that might be—for example, the decriminalization of possession of small amounts of marijuana, or teaching intravenous drug users to sterilize their needles.

POLITICIZATION

Many politicians, and certainly those in the new right and conservative movements, have successfully adopted the second approach, that is, the pro-family, Just Say No position. It makes them appear to care about social ills and law and order. Yet they do not ask for large appropriations to fight social problems. Despite the Reagan administration's pronouncements on drugs, it has asked for a reduction in the relatively small amounts of money committed to the war on drugs, and it has not supported funding for addiction treatment. Paradoxically, those individuals who generally oppose the new right also participate in the antidrug frenzy, as did the Democrats in Congress during discussions of the antidrug crusade bill in October 1986. Fighting illicit drugs is safe. There are constituencies for tobacco, alcohol, and guns, but none for drugs. Even the drug users tend to be repentant deviants who do not publicly champion the use of drugs. For more than a decade, such associations as the National Organization for the Reform of Marijuana Laws (NORML) have looked at the numbers—the 62 million Americans who have ever used marijuana (not to mention the 5 million to 6 million who have tried it within the last month)—and have imagined that these people would give political clout to their cause.[1] But there has been no uprising by this group against the criminalization of drug use.

Consequently, protesting in support of drug users has been left either in the hands of an organization like NORML, which can easily be characterized as a fringe group, or in the chilly hands of civil liberty groups that struggle for principles without burning for the specific issue. A similar situation prevailed for AIDS until recently, when publicity about the possible spread of the disease to the heterosexual community began to affect the population at large. If protests by gay rights organizations were noticed at all, they were seen as giving politicians a chance to make some vague, tolerant response and then to follow it up with a moral, pro-family statement. And who can imagine a protest by intravenous drug users? Under such conditions it is easy to call for greater attention to the rights of the majority. Those people not involved in drug use or sexual deviancies are being rallied against those who are presumed to be a threat. Because there is so little political opposition, little attention must be paid to showing that such a threat exists.

THE CONNECTION BETWEEN AIDS AND DRUG USE

With the obvious exception of intravenous drug users, there is no rational connection between AIDS victims and other drug users. Unfortunately, however, this is not a rational universe. If it were, to quote Rita Mae Brown, "It would be men who rode side saddle."[2] My speculation that the two issues are linked in the public mind is not based on any research evidence, but interviews that did not deal directly with this issue have turned up a striking connection.

This impression is understandable. The frequency with which statements about AIDS list homosexual activity and intravenous drug use as its leading causes builds up an association. Further, many Americans, particularly the less sophisticated, believe that homosexual activity is

1. H. Levine and C. Reinarman, "What's Behind 'Jar Wars,'" *The Nation*, March 28, 1987, pp. 388–90.

2. Rita Mae Brown, *Ruby Fruit Jungle* (Plainfield, Vt.: Daughters, Inc., 1973).

conducted in an atmosphere of lasciviousness that includes the abandoned use of alcohol and drugs. These notions center AIDS in a lifestyle that is certainly unconventional and usually abhorrent.

The connection was strengthened when an official White House spokesman, Carlton Turner, was reported by *Newsweek* as speculating that marijuana use may lead to homosexuality.[3] Turner and other White House spokesmen have also referred to the old steppingstone theory of drug use, which has been disproved many times but still retains currency. According to this theory, drug use is progressive in the sense that users need stronger and stronger drugs to get the same effect. Thus regardless of the mildness of their first drug, users are bound to end up injecting heroin. This view ignores the fact that the various types of illicit drugs have very different structures and very different effects, and that they appeal to different types of people. This steppingstone theory, which would justify an assault on all drug use, strengthens the presumed linkage between drug use and AIDS. There also hovers in the background a vague sense that "these people" have deviated from the reigning cultural outlook and are not worthy of the interest and passion needed to protect their civil rights.

Hysteria about Contagion and Risk

Fear is an invitation to the irrational. When danger stirs up the power of the imagination to embellish and enhance, rational explanations lose effectiveness. For example, it doesn't help people who are afraid to fly to tell them that they are far safer in an airplane than they are when driving in their cars near their own homes. Nevertheless, education and dissemination of knowledge do have an impact on irrational fear. If that knowledge is to change reactions and influence behavior, however, the society has to be ready to distinguish between what can be demonstrated as true and the hysteria prompted by fear. So far our society has been unable to set hysteria aside and to accept the facts about both drug use and AIDS.

For AIDS there is a great deal of factual evidence—as outlined two years ago in an article in the *Journal of the American Medical Association*—that the disease can be spread only in three specific ways: sexually, by the accidental injection of contaminated blood, or from mother to

3. *Newsweek*, October 27, 1986, p. 95.

fetus.[4] The second way, the injection of contaminated blood accidentally (for example, by a health care worker), has hardly ever occurred. It is so rare that there is only one documented case in Britain—that of a nurse who acquired the virus after receiving a microinjection of blood following an arterial puncture. In the three other cases reported in the United States, it is possible that the virus was not acquired through injection but by one of the other two routes. The difficulty of acquiring the infection accidentally is shown by a study of more than 660 subjects who received accidental needle sticks from infected needles; of these, although one acquired hepatitis B, none picked up the AIDS virus.[5]

A later editorial in the *New England Journal of Medicine* says that "the epidemic of acquired immunodeficiency syndrome (AIDS) has become an epidemic of fear."[6] The editorial points out that scientific evidence taken out of context has been used to further the hysteria. For example, the fact that evidence of the virus was found in sweat, tears, and saliva led some people, even some health care workers, to shun those known to be HIV positive even though it was shown that the virus in sweat, tears, or saliva was of too low a concentration to infect and that there were no cases of AIDS acquired by these routes. Yet, as a result of this fear, U.S. dentists and technicians are routinely wearing rubber gloves, which are now in short supply worldwide. Michael A. Jenike of Massachusetts General Hospital reports in an article intriguingly headed, "Mosquitoes Don't Wear Condoms," that fear of AIDS has become an incapacitating disease for some and an impediment to living for many.[7] There is no doubt that the grim reality of an inevitable, painful death from the disease warrants great concern and every rational precautionary measure, including lifestyle changes for many;

4. D. P. Francis and J. Chin, "The Prevention of Acquired Immunodeficiency Syndrome in the United States: An Objective Strategy for Medicine, Public Health, Business, and the Community," *Journal of the American Medical Association*, vol. 257 (March 1987), pp. 1357–66.

5. G. H. Friedland and others, "Lack of Transmission of HTLV-III LAV Infection to Household Contacts of Patients with AIDS or AIDS-related Complex with Oral Candidiasis," *New England Journal of Medicine*, vol. 314 (February 1986), pp. 344–49.

6. J. E. Osborn, "AIDS: Politics and Science," *New England Journal of Medicine*, vol. 318 (February 1988), pp. 444–47.

7. Michael A. Jenike, "Mosquitoes Don't Wear Condoms: When Fear of AIDS Becomes a Disease," *Psychiatric Times*, vol. 4 (November 1987), pp. 6, 7.

but the current hysteria is unwarranted and can only lead to polariza-tion and prosecution.

Under these conditions it tends to be forgotten that the test for the AIDS virus or, more accurately, for the antibody reaction to the virus, which is what actually shows up in the test—performs best when the condition being looked for is relatively common. The test is less accurate when the condition is rare. Let us say that at its best this test (usually the one known as ELISA) produces only two false positives for every 1,000 people who are *not* infected.[8] Test a population of 100,000 with no infections, and 200 false positives will emerge. Another population of the same size with 100 infected people will produce the same 200 false positives, but the test would detect 99 true positives and miss one; thus in this population in which the infection rate is relatively low, two-thirds of the positive results would be false. In a third population of 100,000 with 10,000 infected people, the test would detect 9,900 cases of infection while missing 100, with only 180 false positives: the percentage of false positives now drops below 2 percent. These numbers reveal the value of testing those at high risk from the known routes of infection and perhaps, under some circumstances, for testing those at low risk. Generally, the only ones able to judge the degree of risk are the subjects. But these numbers also show the enormous confusion that could be generated if so-called convenience testing, such as that of couples applying for a marriage license, was to be mandated. Potential risk must be ascertained rationally, not hysteri-cally, if a genuine assessment of the possibilities of contagion is to be made.

Can the risk of AIDS be reduced to zero for people who are sexually active and have not been monogamous over the last eight years? Probably not quite to zero, but close enough to provide a sense of security if people use condoms and show reasonable care in the choice of sexual partners. A program aimed at preventing the spread of AIDS first needs to reduce the hysteria so that information such as this can be absorbed and acted on.

A similar atmosphere of hysteria pervades the illicit drug scene. The Reagan war on drugs, which follows several other wars on drugs, proceeds even though the use of all drugs, including alcohol, has

8. M. J. Barry, "AIDS Tests: When and for Whom?" *Harvard Medical School Health Letter*, September 1987, pp. 5–8.

declined since 1979, with the possible exception of cocaine.[9] As with AIDS, there is no doubt that the abuse of illegal drugs causes serious social, health, and economic difficulties. To dispel the hysteria, three matters must be considered: first, just how great the damage from drug use is; second, to what extent (as with AIDS) an excessive emotional response impedes rather than helps the implementation of effective damage control measures; and, third, what better ways there are to deal with the situation.

Is damage to be defined as any drug use at all, or as the disastrous consequences of drug abuse? If damage refers to these disastrous consequences, the first order of business is to differentiate among the substances that are being used. It is estimated that well over 90 percent of those individuals who smoke tobacco regularly for more than a month will become addicted, while fewer than 1 percent of regular marijuana users become addicted (defined as smoking several times a day). The figure for alcohol is in the 5 percent to 9 percent range. It has been hard to make even informed guesses about the percentage of occasional users of cocaine and opiates who become addicts. Some experts say 10 to 20 percent of occasional users of cocaine become addicts. The figure is probably lower for users of opiates.[10] A more interesting figure might be the estimated 600 cocaine-related deaths last year. Many include use of other drugs, in contrast to the estimate of more than 300,000 tobacco-related fatalities: a ratio of 1 to 500.[11] Not one case of genuine addiction has been reported for psychedelic drugs.[12]

9. L. D. Johnston, P. M. O'Malley, and J. G. Bachman, *National Trends in Drug Use and Related Factors among American High School Students and Young Adults, 1975–1986,* DHHS Publication (ADM) 87-1535 (Government Printing Office, 1987).

10. N. J. Kozel and E. H. Adams, eds., "Cocaine Use in America: Epidemiologic and Clinical Perspectives," National Institute on Drug Abuse, Research Monograph 61 (Government Printing Office, 1985); S. M. Mirin and R. D. Weiss, *Cocaine* (Ballantine Press, 1987); M. S. Burglass, "The Use of Marijuana and Alcohol by Regular Users of Cocaine: Patterns of Use and Style of Control," in H. B. Milkman and H. J. Shaffer, eds. *The Addictions* (D.C. Heath and Company, 1983), pp. 111–20.

11. H. Levine and C. Reinarman, "The Monkey on the Public's Back," *New York Newsday,* January 4, 1987.

12. Norman E. Zinberg, *Drug, Set, and Setting: The Basis for Controlled Intoxicant Use* (Yale University Press, 1984).

These percentages indicate risk similar to that which applies to contracting AIDS, although, fortunately, for certain drug users the outcome is far less grim than for AIDS victims. Even in the highest risk category, a fair percentage of users recover. As programs for intoxicated drivers and employment assistance proliferate, a much higher percentage of alcoholics is being reached earlier and treated successfully. Cocaine addicts, who until now have frequently come from middle-class or upper-middle-class backgrounds, respond well to the treatment programs economically available to them once they have taken the step to use them.[13] This situation may change, however, because cocaine use is rapidly moving down the social scale. The next generation of people in trouble with the drug may not only be unable to afford treatment but may also be less accustomed to relying on that form of treatment. After tobacco addicts, heroin addicts may be the most difficult to treat. At the moment, because so little energy and money have gone into experimenting with different methods of heroin treatment, upgrading existing treatment modalities, or providing places in treatment programs for patients (most treatment programs have a waiting list of six months to a year or more) it is hard to know whether this group of addicts is refractory or simply neglected.

Second, the powerful emotional reaction against drug users (as well as AIDS victims) arises from fear of contagion. This problem has no simple solution. Obviously, the opportunity to use drugs is always present.[14] No culture, except that of the northernmost Eskimos, has ever existed without intoxicants. For the last twenty-five years, Americans have experimented actively with a variety of them. According to one theory, this new interest in old intoxicants was fueled by the development of many new licit psychoactive substances, which resulted in a greater awareness of the possibilities of consciousness change. Although almost all use is down today, some intoxicants have maintained their appeal longer than others. The waves of popularity of certain drugs—for example, of psychedelics from 1962 to 1973, of marijuana from 1966 to the present, of heroin from 1969 to 1971, and of cocaine from 1979 to the present—have usually subsided after a certain length of time. It seems to me that such a health term as "epidemic" is a

13. R. B. Millman, "Evaluation and Clinical Management of Cocaine Abusers," *Journal of Clinical Psychiatry*, vol. 49 (February 1988), pp. 27–33.

14. A. T. Weil, *The Natural Mind* (Houghton Mifflin, 1972).

misnomer. The popularity of drug use is more analogous to the popularity of fads like dungeons and dragons, miniature golf, frisbee throwing, sky diving, and other crazes of lesser or greater danger. The fad element lessens once information about the substance is disseminated, and new choices of drugs emerge. This information is spread through social learning, rather than through formal education, which is only part of the process. It was through social learning that users of psychedelics realized in 1973 what the drug experience would be like and thus avoided the painful and frequently disastrous "trips" of the mid-1960s.

Social learning is much influenced by social policy. Policies that exaggerate and distort make it harder, ultimately, to convince people that a drug is dangerous. (Witness the experience of the upper middle class with cocaine, who may try cocaine largely because they believe its dangers have been exaggerated.) Time and a cool head are needed to sort out what is true and what is primarily a policy statement. Prohibition can only be enforced when a population believes that the substance being prohibited should be prohibited. Few people, after a while, supported the Volstead Act prohibiting the use of alcohol, which was originally expected to eliminate 75 percent of the crime, poverty, and broken homes in the United States.[15] However, few people today would support the legalization of heroin as an intoxicant. This social awareness goes deeper than that revealed by the polls.

An example of deeper social awareness is the changed attitude toward drunk driving. Though many people who drink acknowledge that they have driven when they shouldn't have, few contend that they can drive as well after as before drinking. They increasingly accept DWI (driving while intoxicated) enforcement because they know it is reasonable. Unfortunately, it has taken a long time for that knowledge to be translated into action.

The notion of contagion is particularly disquieting when viewed in terms of class structure. When poverty, ignorance, and despair exist, strange conditions flourish. Old studies by Lee N. Robins showed what could happen when heroin was introduced to a population of young,

---

15. H. G. Levine, "The Alcohol Problem in America: From Temperance to Alcoholism," *British Journal of Addiction*, vol. 79 (March 1984), pp. 109–19.

black, unemployed males.[16] Today the same group is finding cocaine and crack increasingly attractive. If we are concerned for health and safety, we should ask how much of our resources are being put into social programs aimed at those most likely to be at risk. The concepts of social choice and law enforcement have a very different meaning psychologically for those who are most at risk than they have for the employed or educated who nevertheless are often the targets of mandatory testing.

Third, the best way to deal with these very real problems of contagion and risk in drug use is, first of all, to adopt a more sober, less hysterical, and more pragmatic approach. This approach requires a retreat from moralizing and a sharper assessment of social costs. One of the social costs of intravenous drug use is the spread of AIDS, and according to a conservative estimate the cost of AIDS patients in New York City in 1991 will reach $2 billion.[17] In this situation it is not only pathetic but brutal that the subject of a sterile needle exchange program for intravenous drug users, which has been successful in Holland, is less likely to be accepted here because it is seen as condoning drug use. Attitudes must change if a better social climate is to be achieved for the control of both AIDS and drug use.

The Criminalization of Drug Use and AIDS

The criminalization of drug use in the United States was initiated by some of the states before 1914.[18] It became official federal government policy with the passage of the Harrison Narcotic Act in that year and the subsequent Supreme Court decisions upholding it. (As is well known, England at approximately the same time chose to treat addiction as a medical problem, resulting in a very different history.[19]) U.S.

16. L. N. Robins and G. E. Murphy, "Drug Use in a Normal Population of Young Negro Men," *American Journal of Public Health*, vol. 57 (September 1967), pp. 1580–96.

17. P. M. Boffey, "AIDS Panel Calls for Major Effort on Drug Abuse and Health Care," *New York Times*, February 25, 1988.

18. D. F. Musto, *The American Disease: Origins of Narcotic Controls* (Yale University Press, 1973).

19. Norman E. Zinberg and J. A. Robertson, *Drugs and the Public* (Simon and Schuster, 1972).

policy has vacillated since 1914. Some morphine maintenance clinics continued to flourish until 1923; one reported great success until federal agents forced it out of business.[20] In 1929 a movement to treat prisoners with addiction problems got under way, and in the early 1930s some successful experiments were conducted that ended because of World War II.

Heroin use increased in 1953. In 1956 the federal government announced a tough criminal approach to the problem, mandating sentences of five years for the first offense, ten years for the second, and twenty years to life for the third, with no parole. This phase lasted until 1966, when many of the same congressmen and senators who had passed the first law sponsored the act that repealed it, the Narcotic Addict Rehabilitation Act. By then it had become clear that the severity of the first law had reduced its effectiveness. The Rehabilitation Act offered the remedy of civil commitment under the sponsorship of the federal government. The Rehabilitation Act, which wasn't officially repealed until 1972, included provisions for treatment centers, but the Nixon administration abandoned that idea as too expensive and too cumbersome.

At about the same time New York state passed the Rockefeller drug law, again mandating long, fixed sentences, no parole, and little judicial discretion. This law was seen as an experiment for the nation and was much heralded as finally taking the offensive in the war against drug abuse. But just as opponents had claimed, neither the court system, the public, the law enforcement system, nor the prison system could handle its implementation. A careful study by the New York City Bar Association documented the failure of the law to do what it had set out to do. The study showed that fewer arrests and convictions occurred than before passage of the law and that drug use continued to flourish.[21]

In 1981 the Reagan administration initiated a program including block grants to the state, thus returning the assault on drug use to local control. That effort was a thinly disguised way of reducing the

20. D. Waldorf, M. Orlick, and C. Reinarman, *Morphine Maintenance: The Shreveport Clinic 1919–1923*, Special Series 1 (Washington, D.C.: Drug Abuse Council, 1974).

21. Association of the Bar of the City of New York, *The Effects of the 1973 Drug Laws on the New York State Courts* (New York: Association of the Bar of the City of New York, 1976).

investment in the struggle against drug abuse, particularly the money for treatment. The summer and fall of 1986 saw one more drug bill hammered out in the usual atmosphere of hysteria, but the intentions of the lawmakers were poorly thought through, and little came of this ineffective bill.

Now the Reagan administration is attempting, by mandatory testing, to apply some of the same law-enforcement methods to attack or prevent drug use. The rhetoric has changed somewhat to focus on health, safety, and productivity. But, as Allan Adler pointed out at the October 1987 Brookings conference, when President Reagan uses the term "drug testing" in his Executive Order and when the president's organized crime commission talks about mandatory drug testing, such testing is seen as an adjunct to ongoing criminal law-enforcement interdiction efforts. Mandatory drug testing is characterized as the demand-side effort to complement the supply-side interdiction effort.

The members of the Reagan administration should of course pay attention to health, safety, and productivity in the workplace. However, concentrating on a potential law-enforcement effort may not only result in going after the wrong people but may create a Prohibition-like mentality. During the Prohibition era many respectable citizens patronized bootleggers and became criminals; police and public officials were corrupted as never before. Something like this has already happened with regard to drug use, and mandatory urinalysis could result in the adulteration of urines, the corruption of test overseers, or the falsification of test results. The assault on jobs indeed hits people where they live. Those for whom drug use is a fairly inconsequential matter will be influenced by their fear of urine testing. For heavier users, however, such a testing program will only stretch their ingenuity and create a more confrontational atmosphere in our society.

Although there is talk about guaranteeing confidentiality, the federal guidelines for mandatory testing show clear signs that confidentiality takes second place if lawbreaking is suspected. The guidelines refer to the Privacy Act, and a Privacy Act System of Records is to be established to cover both the agency's and the contractor's records of employee urinalysis test results. Although these guidelines are incredibly detailed in other areas, for protection of privacy the document only says that the records are to be maintained and used with the highest regard for employee privacy, and that the Secretary [of Health and Human Services] may make changes in the guidelines to reflect improvement in science and technology. According to *Of Substance*, a newsletter of the Legal Action Center of the city of New York, there are many ways in which the federal regulations can be bypassed without client consent.[22] Sometimes they can be bypassed for supposedly benign reasons, such as to ensure the payment of benefits, but at other times the reason may reflect the intense desires of authorities, employees, or others to obtain information.

In this climate of hysteria, the arguments of health and safety that are used to justify mandatory testing for drug use can also be used to justify testing for AIDS. Mandatory testing for AIDS would lead to criminalizing the issue as well.[23] Proposals have already been made to prosecute those who know they have AIDS for acts that could lead to transmission of the disease. At the Brookings October 1987 conference, Congressman William E. Dannemeyer, Republican of California, claimed that because the failure to report certain other sexually transmitted diseases was accepted as a crime, the same should be true for AIDS. He overlooked the original reason for the reporting of other diseases, which was to institute treatment. Since AIDS is incurable, that is not the reason in this case. In the present climate of fear and hysteria, people known to have AIDS are regarded as worse than lepers: consider, for example, the persecution of the children with hemophilia who contracted AIDS.

Civil Liberties

The civil liberties aspect of testing presents enormous difficulties. Does mandatory testing for either drug use or AIDS deprive individuals of equal treatment by law? So far court decisions about drug testing have been more protective of federal employees than they have been of employees of private companies. Great concern has also been shown about protecting the rights of those with false positives. Ian Macdonald, in his presentation, dealt with that issue by giving figures indicating the stunning accuracy of the Army testing program, but he failed to

22. Legal Action Center of the City of New York, *Of Substance*, a newsletter for the substance abuse treatment community, January-February 1987 and March-April 1987.

23. M. A. R. Kleiman and R. A. Mockler, *AIDS and Heroin: Strategies for Control* (Washington, D.C.: Urban Institute Press, October 1988).

mention that to achieve that accuracy the Army had changed the testing process so that now a positive is triggered by 100 nannograms. Formerly, 50 nannograms triggered a positive. These new guidelines avoid the inequity of false positives but present us with the different inequity of individual idiosyncrasy. It is clear that after using the same amount of the same drug, some individuals retain higher concentrations in their urine than others do. Consequently under the Army program some individuals will be caught and punished for the same crime for which others will go free.

As Allan Adler pointed out in the Brookings conference, for both AIDS and drug use, the purpose of the testing is to identify people, to single them out—and then what? Remember that the test for AIDS tests for the antibodies that respond to the AIDS virus, not for the virus itself, and that for some time (some weeks or months) after infection, the individual will be test negative until the antibodies develop. In the same way, the tests for drug use only pick up metabolites of the substances and do not test directly for the substances themselves. Certainly those individuals who have AIDS are incurably ill and are a tremendous health burden; but those who are HIV positive may never get the disease, although they do represent a risk. To what extent will they be subjected to prejudice and discrimination, as opposed to education and counseling? Individuals whose test results are false positives will also become targets for discrimination, and that attitude toward them will not change much even if later it should become known that the positive was false. In effect, under this testing program all drug users may be charged with being either a health and safety hazard or a detriment to productive work. Those charges could be addressed if they were indeed the only ones, but the users will face criminal charges too. Are these difficulties outweighed or at least balanced by the effectiveness of the testing, the likelihood that testing will achieve its desired end of prevention, and the assurance that the same aims could not be achieved by other means less destructive to individual rights? The proponents of mandatory testing must be prepared to answer these questions.

If in addressing the issues of civil liberties one thinks of privacy alone, it is easy to forget the extent to which the Constitution protects that right. During the hearings that led to the Senate's refusal to confirm Judge Robert Bork as a justice of the Supreme Court, many Americans rediscovered the protection of freedom of speech and belief as well as the protection against unreasonable searches and seizures and the guarantees against self-incrimination. All of these shelter an individual's right to a private, inviolable space both physically and psychologically. Combined with the doctrine of presumption of innocence stressed by Allan Adler, these rights should provide a powerful wall of protection. Numerous high court decisions support this wall of rights, although many of these decisions seem to define the key words, such as "reasonable," acting in such a way as to limit the absolute nature of an individual's right to privacy.

The often-quoted U.S. Supreme Court decision in the case of *Warden* v. *Hayden* (1967), which states that confidentiality is not guaranteed, also says that if there is a belief that a crime has been committed and that the evidence has been concealed, a search warrant will override any privacy claim.[24] Would a decision such as this apply to mandatory urinalysis as a test for drug use or AIDS? How much evidence of possible illegal drug taking and the concealment of the evidence in the body is needed to meet those requirements? To take a specific case, if a certain behavior by someone who is HIV positive is considered illegal, to what extent would it be the responsibility of that individual to ascertain his or her potential for HIV positivity? This case only suggests the types of labyrinthian legal issues that will be raised by any notion of mandatory testing for either drugs or AIDS. The struggle over these same issues is so bitter and the opinions as to a reasonable solution so divided that many of these questions will have to be decided by the courts.

INTRAVENOUS DRUG USE AND AIDS

Intravenous drug users are, after gay men, the second largest group likely to be carriers of AIDS. This group may also be responsible for the explosive growth of AIDS within the heterosexual population. On August 21, 1986, barely 1 percent of heterosexual intravenous drug users in San Francisco had AIDS (twenty-eight cases); but about the same time more than 90 percent of a general sample of intravenous drug users acknowledged having recently shared hypodermic equipment, an action linked to the possibility for rapid contagion, and fully

24. *Warden* v. *Hayden* 387 U. S. 294 (1967).

16 percent of that sample tested positive for AIDS.[25] Yet the general HIV-positive rate for intravenous drug users in San Francisco was but 9 percent, compared with a reported 45 percent in New York City. The long, uncertain incubation period of AIDS suggests the hypothesis that the original, more widespread transmission of the disease through intravenous drug users began later than the transmission through men engaged in frequent receptive anal intercourse, but that it may soon begin to catch up.

To understand what makes people decide to try intoxicants, how these intoxicants affect them, and how use develops over time, three interlocking variables must be considered: the pharmacological properties of the drug; the set, that is, the values, attitudes, and personality structure of the user; and the influence of the physical and social setting in which use takes place. Until recently this third variable has been the least understood.[26]

Since the drug revolution of 1961–62, our knowledge of the effect of the drug itself has been increased vastly by in vitro and animal experimentation research and, to a lesser extent, by in vivo work. At the extreme of toxicity the research can tell us much about the effect of drug use on humans. Less impressive work has been done on the personality (set) of the user. Some of these efforts seem to show certain psychological vulnerabilities that could predict a potential for addiction by certain individuals. Although such individuals can be found, that view hardly accounts for the large numbers of users who get into serious trouble with intoxicants, as George Vaillant and others have demonstrated.[27] Nor does it add much to our understanding of the far greater number who use intoxicants in a variety of ways without getting into serious trouble or becoming addicted. Finally, some work has been done on the

25. J. A. Newmeyer, "HIV Infection and Risk Factors among Intravenous Drug Users in San Francisco," paper presented at the American Public Health Association, Las Vegas, Nevada, October 1986.

26. Zinberg, *Drug, Set, and Setting.*

27. George E. Vaillant, *The Natural History of Alcoholism: Course, Patterns, and Paths to Recovery* (Harvard University Press, 1983); J. A. Clausen, "Drug Addictions: Social Aspects," in D. Sills, ed., *International Encyclopedia of the Social Sciences*, vol. 4 (Macmillan, 1968); and H. J. Shaffer and B. Gambino, "Addiction Paradigms II: Theory, Research, and Practice," *Journal of Psychedelic Drugs*, vol. 11 (October-December 1979), pp. 299–304.

social factors that influence drug use, such as a broken home or the loss of the mother at an early age. But since the purpose of such research is to show the effect of social elements on the development of psychological vulnerability, it is really concerned with the personality of the user rather than the social setting surrounding use.

The social setting is critical in determining how intoxicants are used and how social policy is formulated and becomes effective. Certain social conditions are also at work at this time. Recent concerns about weight—alcohol contains many calories and marijuana gives one the "munchies"—are influential, as is the current interest in health and exercise. The point is that at this moment powerful forces for moderation indicate that a realistic move can be made toward preventing misuse and its disastrous effects on health. Yet at the same time government policy has once more declared war on drugs, attempting, unrealistically, to prevent all use by adopting a prohibitionistic attitude that ignores the great divide between controlled and compulsive use. This policy, personified by Nancy Reagan, most of network television, and the frenzied 1986 drug bill, has immediate and dangerous implications for the spread of AIDS.

To cite one example, in Massachusetts a recent Request for Proposal issued by the Department of Public Health for all the state-funded methadone maintenance clinics limits the methadone treatment of patients to eighteen months and will provide only a few slots for patients remaining in treatment that long.[28] In effect this proposal turns methadone "maintenance" into a detoxification program, leaving this chronic "disease" treatable only by abstinence, which can be effective for just a small fraction of those currently in treatment. Such a social policy will force a good percentage of those dropped from long-term methadone maintenance, and probably most of them, back onto the street for their drugs and needles. We can expect, on the basis of a study made recently in San Francisco, that as many as 90 percent of these users will not have their needles sterilized for AIDS. In this country AIDS is already of epidemic proportions; surely we do not need a social policy that, conceiving of methadone as a "drug," puts heroin users back on the street and thus unwittingly contributes to the further

28. Massachusetts Department of Public Health, Division of Alcoholism and Drug Rehabilitation, Request for Funding Proposal (RFP), fiscal year 1988, for methadone services, program narrative, treatment model, Fall 1986.

spread of that fatal disease.

In conclusion, I would say that there is a basic need to differentiate between drug use and drug abuse. There is also a need to put the danger of AIDS transmittal by intravenous drug users in proper perspective. The issues associated with testing therefore become secondary to the need for greater emphasis on public education and counseling of those at risk.

Conference Participants

Allan Adler
American Civil Liberties Union

William Alden
Drug Enforcement Administration
U.S. Department of Justice

Betty Jane Anderson*
American Medical Association

Judith Areen
Georgetown University Law Center

Terry Beirn
Committee on Labor and Human Resources
U.S. Senate

Reed Bell
Public Health Service
U.S. Department of Health and Human Services

Meg Bennett*
Whitman-Walker Clinic, Inc.

Karst Besteman
Alcohol and Drug Problems Association

Tom Blau
Hudson Institute

Erwin Bloom
National Institute on Drug Abuse
U.S. Department of Health and Human Services

Edward Botwinick
Timeplex Inc.

William Boyd*
The Johnson Foundation

Jack Bratton
ITT Corporation

Raymond C. Brown*
National Institute of Corrections
U.S. Department of Justice

Robert L. Brutsche
Bureau of Prisons
U.S. Department of Justice

Edward Burger*
Georgetown University Medical Center

William Butynski*
National Association of State Alcohol and Drug Abuse Directors

Warren I. Cikins*
Center for Public Policy Education
Brookings Institution

Marcus Conant
California State Department of Health Task Force on AIDS

William E. Dannemeyer
U.S. Representative
Thirty-Ninth District, California

One asterisk means that the participant attended both conferences. Two asterisks indicate that the participant attended only the conference in Racine, Wisconsin.

Joseph DeRosa*
IC Industries, Corporate Offices

Donna M. Dezenhall*
Center for Public Policy Education
Brookings Institution

Lee Dogoloff
American Council for Drug Education

Jeanne Easton
Dade County Health Department

Stephen Foster
Charles A. Dana Foundation

Rita Goodman**
Johnson Foundation

Hayden Gregory
Committee on the Judiciary
U.S. House of Representatives

Robert Guttman
Subcommittee on Labor
Committee on Labor and Human
Resources
U.S. Senate

Henry Halsted**
The Johnson Foundation

Dick Hays
U.S. Department of Education

John Henning
American Medical Association

Peter Heseltine
University of Southern California

John Hills
Brookings Institution

George Hitchings*
Burroughs Wellcome Fund

Kevin Hopkins
Hudson Institute

Russel Iuculano*
American Council of Life Insurance

Billy Jones*
Whitman-Walker Clinic, Inc.

Nolan Jones*
National Governors' Association

Robert Katzmann
Federal Judicial Center

Richard Kinch**
The Johnson Foundation

Lawrence Kingsley
University of Pittsburgh

Mathilde Krim
American Foundation for AIDS Research

Susan Poulsen Krogh**
The Johnson Foundation

J. Michael Lane
Emory University Medical School

Warren Leiden
American Immigration Lawyers
Association

Carl Leukefeld*
National Institute on Drug Abuse
U.S. Department of Health and Human
Services

Jeffrey Levi
National Gay and Lesbian Task Force

Donald Ian Macdonald
Drug Abuse Policy Office
The White House

Bruce K. MacLaury
Brookings Institution

William L. Marsh
George Washington University Hospital

John Mazzuchi
U.S. Department of Defense

John McKay
Texans' War on Drugs

Richard Merritt
Intergovernmental Health Policy Project

Lawrence Miike
Office of Technology Assessment
U.S. Congress

Kenneth P. Moritsugu**
Bureau of Prisons
U.S. Department of Justice

Mark Newport
Southwestern Bell Publications

June Osborn*
University of Michigan

Sandra Panem
Alfred P. Sloan Foundation

Roy Pickens
National Institute on Drug Abuse
U.S. Department of Health and Human
Services

Beny Primm
Addiction Research and Treatment
Corporation

Peter Reuter*
Rand Corporation

Nancy Rhett
Planning and Evaluation Service
U.S. Department of Education

Timothy R. Schoewe**
Milwaukee Fire and Police Commission

Steve Schorling
Center for Public Policy Education
Brookings Institution

Stephen Schultz
New York City Department of Health

James R. Sevick*
JRS Research and Consulting

Phillip Shellhaas*
IBM Corporation

Robert Shriver
James D. Wolfensohn Inc.

Morton Silverman
Associate Dean of Students in the
University
University of Chicago

Kenneth W. Starr
U.S. Court of Appeals for the District of
Columbia Circuit

Eric Sterling
Subcommittee on Crime
Committee on the Judiciary
U.S. House of Representatives

Florence Sterrett*
Botwinick-Wolfensohn Foundation

James K. Stewart
National Institute of Justice
U.S. Department of Justice

Peggy Taylor
Legislative Department
AFL-CIO

Sir John Thomson
Twenty-first Century Fund

Anthony Travisono*
American Correctional Association

Arnold Trebach
American University

Ronald Valdiserri
University of Pittsburgh

Ivan White
Federal Bureau of Prisons
U.S. Department of Justice

Eric Wish
National Institute of Justice
U.S. Department of Justice

Constance Wofsy
San Francisco General Hospital

Norman Zinberg*
Harvard University